Informational Texts for
Striving Readers

High-Interest Nonfiction Passages
With Comprehension Questions

MICHAEL PRIESTLEY

SCHOLASTIC
Teacher
RESOURCES

ACKNOWLEDGMENTS

For their assistance in the development of this book, the author would like to acknowledge contributions from Sheri Gushta, Cheryl Gracey, Carolyn Mailler, and Adele Priestley.

Photos ©: cover (top left): Mike Schultz/EyeEm/Getty Images; cover (center): Ben Stansall/AFP/Getty Images; 9 (left and right): Francisco Fonturbel; 13 (shipwreck icon): The Noun Project; 15: The Image Bank/Getty Images; 17: Brazil Photo Press/Alamy Stock Photo; 29 (main): Manuscripts and Archives Division, The New York Public Library; 29 (inset): World Archive/Alamy Stock Photo; 31: Look and Learn/Bridgeman Images; 36: Jacques Langevin/Sygma/Sygma/Getty Images; 39: Library of Congress; 47: Satori13/Dreamstime; 57: Jim McMahon/Mapman ®; 59: Richie Lomba/Dreamstime; 66: ullstein bild/ullstein bild/Getty Images; 77 (bottom): Adisha Pramod/Alamy Stock Photo. All other photos © Shutterstock.com.

Editor: Maria L. Chang
Cover design: Tannaz Fassihi
Interior design: Maria Lilja

ISBN: 978-1-338-71466-1
Scholastic Inc., 557 Broadway, New York, NY 10012
Copyright © 2021 by Michael Priestley
Published by Scholastic Inc. All rights reserved.
Printed in the U.S.A.
First printing, January 2021.
1 2 3 4 5 6 7 8 9 10   40   30 29 28 27 26 25 24 23 22 21

CONTENTS

Using Sources

Reasons and Evidence

Integrating Information

Social Studies and Science Texts

Practice Test

A NOTE TO TEACHERS

Welcome to *Informational Texts for Striving Readers: Grade 5*. Inside this book you'll find 30 reading passages designed to engage students and help increase their comprehension skills. The high-interest texts include a variety of informational articles and some literary nonfiction (see sidebar). All the passages feature grade-appropriate content written at relatively low readability levels, ranging from Grade 4.0 to 5.5 (between 500L and 800L, based on the Lexile measures). Generally, passages at the beginning are the easiest, with the difficulty level gradually increasing as you progress through the book.

The passages are organized in ten chapters that focus on core reading standards and comprehension skills. Each passage comes with comprehension questions in a variety of formats, including multiple choice, multiple response, short answer, two-part evidence-based, text highlighting (sometimes called "hotspot"), sequencing, and matching/comparison tables. These questions help students think about what they have read and make sure they understand it. They also give students practice in answering various types of test questions. Even more important, they can give you assessment data to help you determine how well your students are reading or what kinds of instructional support they might need.

Quick Assessment

For additional assessment, a practice test follows the ten chapters. You'll find the answer key to both the comprehension questions and practice test at the back of the book. Item rationales, which explain why answer choices are correct or incorrect, are part of the answer key.

To score the questions, award each correct response one point. A multiple-choice question is worth one point; a multiple-response item with two correct answers is worth two points. For two-part items, students must answer Part A correctly before they can earn credit for the correct response(s) in Part B. Sequencing items and comparison tables are worth one point each if all answers within the item are correct. For short-answer questions, accept responses that vary from the exact wording in the answer key.

Taking It Further

You can also use some of the passages to have students go beyond answering the questions provided. For example, you might choose to have students write a summary of the text or compose an essay based on one or more passages. For the more challenging texts, students may benefit from discussing them first and then writing about them in a variety of ways.

> ### Informational Text and Literary Nonfiction
>
> According to the Common Core State Standards, informational text "includes biographies and autobiographies; books about history, social studies, science, and the arts; technical texts, including directions, forms, and information displayed in graphs, charts, or maps; and digital sources on a range of topics" (ELA Standard 10: Range of Text Types for K–5). This broad definition also includes all literary nonfiction, such as personal essays, speeches, opinion pieces, and memoirs.

Name: _____   Date: _____

Ice Cream in a Bag

Have you ever made ice cream in a plastic bag? That may sound odd.
But making ice cream at home is easy with this simple recipe.
As an added bonus, you'll even get some exercise.

What You Need

1 cup half-and-half cream
$\frac{1}{2}$ cup fresh berries
1 quart-size zip-lock plastic bag
1 gallon-size zip-lock plastic bag

1 teaspoon vanilla extract
$\frac{1}{4}$ cup sugar
$\frac{1}{2}$ cup salt
4 cups ice

What to Do

1. Put the cream, berries, sugar, and vanilla in the smaller quart-size plastic bag. Seal the bag tightly.
2. Fill the larger gallon-size bag halfway with ice. Add the salt.
3. Put the smaller bag (with the mixture) inside the larger bag with the ice and salt. Close the bag tightly.
4. Shake the bags for five minutes. Wear gloves so your hands don't freeze.
5. When ready, remove the small bag from the larger one. Wash off the salt with cold water.
6. Now, open up the bag and enjoy your ice cream!

Informational Texts for Striving Readers: Grade 5 © 2021 by Michael Priestley, Scholastic Inc. • page 6

1. **Which <u>two</u> things go into the larger bag? Write your answers.**

   _____

2. **When making ice cream, you should use gloves to —**

   (A) protect your skin from the salt   (C) avoid crushing the berries

   (B) keep the bag from breaking   (D) keep your hands warm

3. **Which kind of ice cream can you make with this recipe?**

   (A) lemon   (C) chocolate

   (B) strawberry   (D) peanut butter

Name: _____   Date: _____

Climbing El Capitan

Every year, hundreds of climbers try to reach the top of El Capitan.

Informational Texts for Striving Readers: Grade 5 © 2021 by Michael Priestley, Scholastic Inc. • page 7

1   The stunning beauty of Yosemite National Park in California draws more than 4 million visitors each year. As you enter the Yosemite Valley, the first thing you notice is "El Capitan." It is one of the tallest rock walls in the world. Made of sheer granite, it rises more than 3,000 feet. That's two and a half times the height of the Empire State Building!

2   If you look closely at El Capitan, you might see small, dark spots moving up the wall. These are rock climbers. For years, people thought El Capitan was impossible to climb. Now it is one of the most popular rock-climbing spots in the world.

3   Climbing El Capitan is not easy. It takes most people three to five days to reach the top. Some routes take even longer. That means climbers must carry a lot of food and water. They also need a "portaledge" for sleeping. This device is like a tent made of metal bars. A climber hangs it from the rock wall and sleeps inside it. The food, water, and gear add extra weight for the climber to carry.

4   In 1993, Lynn Hill became the first person to free-climb "The Nose." That is one of the most famous routes to the top. Free climbers use safety ropes to protect them if they fall. But they don't have any helpers. They climb alone and do all of the work themselves. One year later, Hill climbed The Nose again. This time she did it in less than a day. Only two people have ever climbed it that fast.

(continued)

5   In 2017, a climber named Alex Hannold broke another record. He shocked the world by climbing El Capitan *without* ropes. No one had ever done that before! He scaled the wall in 3 hours and 56 minutes. If he had fallen, no safety gear would have saved him. But he reached the top safely—and made history.

6   Every year, new climbers push the boundaries in Yosemite. We can only wonder who will make climbing history next on the famous walls of El Capitan.

1. **Which sentences from the passage tell why so many climbers are attracted to El Capitan? Choose <u>two</u> answers.**

    (A) "As you enter the Yosemite Valley, the first thing you notice is 'El Capitan.'"

    (B) "It is one of the tallest rock walls in the world."

    (C) "For years, people thought El Capitan was impossible to climb."

    (D) "Climbing El Capitan is not easy."

    (E) "It takes most people three to five days to reach the top."

2. **Based on the passage, why is a multi-day climb challenging for climbers?**

    (A) They miss their family and friends.

    (B) They get bored and lose concentration.

    (C) They have to carry a lot of extra weight.

    (D) They cannot sleep until they reach the top.

3. **What did Alex Hannold do that no one had ever done before? Write your answer.**

    _____

    _____

Name: _____ Date: _____

The Little Monkey of the Mountain

The *monito del monte* is so small, it can hang from a human finger.

1   Have you ever heard of the *monito del monte*? It is a special animal that lives only in parts of South America. In English, its name means "little monkey of the mountain." But this little critter is not a monkey!

2   The *monito del monte* is a marsupial. The marsupials are a unique family of animals. Like mammals, they take care of their babies until the babies can feed themselves. But a marsupial mother carries her baby in a pouch. The pouch is like a pocket on her body. Kangaroos and koalas are other examples of marsupials. They live in Australia. The only marsupial native to North America is the opossum.

3   So why is the *monito del monte* so special? It is the smallest marsupial in the world! It has gray fur, small ears, and a long tail. It looks like a mouse. Its body (without the tail) is only three to five inches long. It can fit in one of your hands!

4   The *monito del monte* lives in the forest. It can climb trees. It builds a nest with leaves and eats insects. It is also *nocturnal*, so it sleeps during the day and is active at night.

5   Sadly, the *monito del monte* is in danger. There aren't very many of them left on Earth. If we humans don't help protect them, they could disappear forever.

The Little Monkey of the Mountain

1. **Which statements about marsupials are <u>true</u>? Choose <u>two</u> answers.**

   (A) Most marsupials live near the ocean.

   (B) Kangaroos and koalas are both marsupials.

   (C) Marsupials carry their babies in pouches.

   (D) Marsupials eat only fruits and vegetables.

   (E) Monkeys and marsupials are the same thing.

2. On what continent does the *monito del monte* live?

   _____

3. **Which sentence from the passage explains why the *monito del monte* is special?**

   (A) "In English, its name means 'little monkey of the mountain.'"

   (B) "It is the smallest marsupial in the world!"

   (C) "It has gray fur, small ears, and a long tail."

   (D) "It is also *nocturnal*, so it sleeps during the day and is active at night."

4. **Which sentences describe the *monito del monte*? Choose <u>two</u> answers.**

   (A) It eats insects.   (D) It has horns.

   (B) It can fly.   (E) It is nocturnal.

   (C) It is blind.

Name: _____ Date: _____

Sailing for Change

Greta Thunberg sailed from England to New York aboard an eco-friendly racing yacht.

1   What is the fastest way to cross the Atlantic Ocean—by plane or by boat? For Greta Thunberg, that was the wrong question. Instead, she asked, "Which way causes less pollution?"

2   Greta grew up in Sweden. When she was 8, she heard about climate change. She learned that using fuels like gas and oil heats up the planet. It causes Earth to get warmer. This changes our climate. Greta wanted to do something.

3   When she was 15, she took action. She made a large sign that said, "SCHOOL STRIKE FOR CLIMATE." Then she sat outside with her sign each Friday. She did not go to school. Newspapers wrote about her. She was on TV. Then she made speeches. She became famous.

4   She spoke to important leaders. She told them about climate change. She urged them to take action. Soon, people around the world paid attention to Greta.

5   At age 16, Greta had an important date. The United Nations asked her to speak about climate change. She made plans to go to New York City.

6   Most people fly across the ocean, but not Greta. An airplane uses a lot of fuel. So she decided to sail to the United States. The boat she chose had solar panels. It used energy from the sun. Wind power moved it forward. The trip took about two weeks. She wanted to show people how to use less fuel.

7   Greta left England on August 14, 2019. Fifteen days later, crowds met her in New York and cheered for her. She told them to help stop climate change. She said, "Let's not wait any longer. Let's do it now."

Sailing for Change

1. **What is Greta Thunberg most worried about?**
   - (A) traveling
   - (B) climate change
   - (C) school strikes
   - (D) the United Nations

2. **What did Greta do to help the climate when she was 15? Name <u>two</u> things.**

   _____

   _____

3. **Which sentence from the passage tells why Greta went to New York?**
   - (A) "Soon, people around the world paid attention to Greta."
   - (B) "At age 16, Greta had an important date."
   - (C) "The United Nations asked her to speak about climate change."
   - (D) "She made plans to go to New York City."

4. **What is the central idea of this passage?**
   - (A) Burning fuels like gas and oil makes Earth warmer.
   - (B) Greta Thunberg knows that airplanes burn a lot of fuel.
   - (C) It took about two weeks to cross the Atlantic Ocean.
   - (D) Greta Thunberg showed people how to act on climate change.

5. **Which sentence from the last paragraph supports the idea that many people liked Greta's ideas? Underline the sentence.**

   Greta left England on August 14, 2019. Fifteen days later, crowds met her in New York and cheered for her. She told them to help stop climate change. She said, "Let's not wait any longer. Let's do it now."

Informational Texts for Striving Readers: Grade 5 © 2021 by Michael Priestley, Scholastic Inc. • page 12

Name: _____ Date: _____

A Sunken Treasure

1   People have told tales of treasures lost at sea for hundreds of years. Few actual treasures are ever found. But, in 1988, explorers found the wreck of the *S.S Central America*. This steamship sank off the coast of South Carolina in 1857. It held one of the greatest lost treasures in U.S. history.

2   In 1857, the California Gold Rush had come to an end. Many people found gold there. They wanted to take it back to the East Coast. At the time, there were no trains to the West. Going by wagon took months. The easiest way to get to the other side of the country was by ship. First, travelers sailed from San Francisco to Panama. Then they crossed Panama by train. From there, they took another ship north to New York. For years, the *S.S. Central America* sailed this last leg of the trip. It made 43 round trips between Panama and New York.

3   On its last trip, the *S.S. Central America* sank in a storm. It was carrying about $400 million worth of gold. At least three tons of gold sank to the ocean floor. And it stayed there for more than 130 years.

4   In 1988, a group led by a man named Tommy Thompson of Ohio spotted the wreck. It was lying on the bottom of the ocean, 7,000 feet deep. Over the next four years, they raised part of the ship's treasure. They found thousands of gold coins and 532 gold bars. Thompson sold most of the loot for $50 million. But there were questions about who owned the treasure.

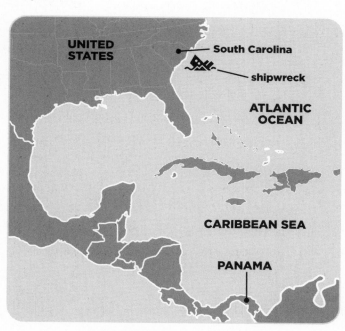

S.S. Central America sank off the coast of South Carolina.

5   In 2014, another group went to the site of the wreck. They brought up more of the treasure. That second haul included 15,500 gold coins and 45 gold bars. Much of the gold went to a company in California—where it all began. The gold went up for sale at a show in 2018. But it cost a lot. A single gold coin cost as much as 1 million dollars. For that price, you got a piece of history, too.

A Sunken Treasure

1. **This question has two parts. Answer Part A. Then answer Part B.**

    PART A **What is the central idea of the passage?**

    (A) Gold coins from a shipwreck went on sale in California in 2018.

    (B) In the 1850s, traveling by ship was easier than going by train or by wagon.

    (C) A lot of gold discovered in California in the 1850s was sent by ship to New York.

    (D) A group of explorers found a sunken ship and its treasure that went down in 1857.

    PART B **Which sentence best supports the central idea from Part A?**

    (A) "People have told tales of treasures lost at sea for hundreds of years."

    (B) "But, in 1988, explorers found the wreck of the *S.S Central America*."

    (C) "It held one of the greatest lost treasures in U.S. history."

    (D) "In 1857, the California Gold Rush had come to an end."

2. **What is paragraph 2 mostly about?**

    (A) where the *S.S. Central America* sailed

    (B) how people traveled across the country

    (C) what happened during the California Gold Rush

    (D) why people went to Panama on the way to New York

3. **Which detail from the passage best supports the idea that the sunken treasure was very valuable?**

    (A) "Many people found gold there. They wanted to take it back to the East Coast."

    (B) "For years, the *S.S. Central America* sailed this last leg of the trip."

    (C) "On its last trip, the *S.S. Central America* sank in a storm. It was carrying about $400 million worth of gold."

    (D) "In 2014, another group went to the site of the wreck."

4. **Which <u>two</u> details should be included in a summary of the passage?**

    (A) In 1857, a ship named *S.S. Central America* sank with a load of gold.

    (B) The *S.S. Central America* made 43 trips between Panama and New York in the 1800s.

    (C) Gold coins and bars found on the *S.S. Central America* went on sale in California in 2018.

    (D) Gold found during the California Gold Rush was carried back to the East Coast on ships like the *S.S. Central America*.

    (E) A group of explorers found the *S.S. Central America* in 1988 and raised millions of dollars' worth of gold from the wreck.

Name: _____ Date: _____

Ancient Cave Art Tells a Story

1. Imagine discovering a painting inside a cave—and finding out it was drawn thousands of years ago! That's what happened in 2017, when some scientists climbed into a cave in Indonesia. This country in Asia is made up of many islands. The cave was on the island of South Sulawesi. Inside the cave, they found a painting that tells a story. They dated the painting at about 44,000 years old! That makes it the oldest known story painting to date.

2. The painting covers a wall about 16 feet long. It shows a hunting scene with several figures chasing animals. Some of the beasts look like animals we see today, such as the dwarf buffalo. Some of the figures look human. But others look like a mix of human and animal. One has a tail. Another has a head shaped like a bird.

Cave painting of a dwarf buffalo

3. Back when the painting was created, people did not have real paints. They used things like charcoal and minerals. They also used a clay that has iron in it. Iron is reddish in color, like rust. This cave art has a lot of red coloring.

4. When scientists discovered the painting, they wanted to know how old it was. They studied mineral growths called "cave popcorn." These growths formed on the painting. Then they measured minerals in the growths. They found *uranium*, which can help determine age. As a result, they noted that some parts of the painting were older than others. This means that different people added to the painting over time. As a whole, the painting ranged from 35,000 to 44,000 years old.

5. That makes this cave painting the oldest example of figurative art found so far. The pictures represent real objects. This shows that people of the time could invent stories.

6. Before this find, scientists believed that the oldest cave paintings were in Europe. But those showed only basic shapes, such as handprints or circles. Story paintings found in Europe are only 10,000 to 20,000 years old. The cave art in Indonesia shows that story painting began much earlier. And it may have started in Asia. Scientists now think that Africa may have some cave paintings we have not yet found. They could be even older than the cave art in Indonesia.

Ancient Cave Art Tells a Story

1. **This question has two parts. Answer Part A. Then answer Part B.**

   PART A **What is the central idea of this passage?**

   (A) Cave art uses natural materials to tell stories about real people and things.

   (B) Scientists believe people in Indonesia could tell stories using handprints and circles.

   (C) An ancient cave painting in Indonesia shows a group of people hunting animals.

   (D) Cave art found in Indonesia provides new information about types of art people made a long time ago.

   PART B **Which sentence best supports the central idea from Part A?**

   (A) "They used things like charcoal and minerals."

   (B) "This cave art has a lot of red coloring."

   (C) "As a result, they noted that some parts of the painting were older than others."

   (D) "That makes this cave painting the oldest example of figurative art found so far."

2. **What is the central idea of paragraph 4?**

   (A) Uranium was found in the cave art in Indonesia.

   (B) Artists like to add new details to existing artwork.

   (C) "Cave popcorn" is the name for growths on a cave wall.

   (D) Scientists used minerals to figure out the age of cave art.

3. **Which two details should be included in a summary of this passage?**

   (A) Artists can use paintings of animals and objects to tell a story.

   (B) Scientists discovered a cave painting in Indonesia that is 44,000 years old.

   (C) Scientists studied minerals on cave walls to figure out the age of the artwork.

   (D) A cave painting found in Indonesia shows ancient humans could tell a story using pictures.

   (E) A cave painting in Indonesia shows a dwarf buffalo, a kind of animal that is still alive today.

4. **Which detail from the passage best supports the idea that people told stories through art?**

   (A) "The painting covers a wall about 16 feet long."

   (B) "It shows several figures chasing animals."

   (C) "But others look like a mix of human and animal."

   (D) "This cave art has a lot of red coloring."

Informational Texts for Striving Readers: Grade 5 © 2021 by Michael Priestley, Scholastic Inc. • page 16

Name: _____ Date: _____

Cirque du Soleil

1   A large yellow and blue tent stands in the middle of a field. Inside, crowds of people sit in the dark. They whisper to one another. Suddenly, colorful lights flash on inside the tent. A group of clowns prance across the floor, their faces painted many colors. A girl wearing a dress covered in jewels and sparkles steps onto the stage. She begins to sing in a dreamy voice. Then acrobats tumble out onto the floor, doing flips and handstands. Their shiny red suits make them look like they are on fire. High in the air, men jump rope on a thin wire. The audience gasps. The circus has come to life.

Lively performers wear dazzling costumes.

2   Cirque du Soleil (SURK du so-LAY) is one of the most famous shows in the world. The name means "Circus of the Sun" in French. This circus features amazing performers, but it has no animal acts. It all started out as a street show in Quebec, Canada. In the early 1980s, a small group of artists wandered the streets of their small town. They performed fancy tricks. They walked on stilts, juggled balls, and danced. The people of the town enjoyed watching them.

3   The show inspired one man, Guy Laliberté. He was a performer. He dreamed of a circus that would travel all over the world. He organized the group of street artists. He took them to perform at festivals. Some banks and big companies lent him money. He got support from the government. In 1984, the group became Cirque du Soleil.

4   At first, the group had 73 people. By 2019, it had 4,000 employees from 50 countries. The performers are the best at what they do. Many of them were great athletes before they joined the circus. All of the details of the show—the music, makeup, dances—are chosen carefully. Together, they create a masterpiece.

5   Cirque du Soleil started small. But over the past 30 years, it has performed in more than 400 cities around the world. More than 180 million people have seen its shows. The shows bring in more than $1 billion of sales each year. And they continue to spread joy and magic to their audience.

Cirque du Soleil

1. **Which kind of act would people most likely see at a Cirque du Soleil show?**

   (A) lion taming

   (B) elephant tricks

   (C) talking puppets

   (D) tightrope walking

2. **Which words best describe the costumes of Cirque du Soleil performers? Choose two answers.**

   (A) safe

   (B) colorful

   (C) simple

   (D) plain

   (E) exciting

3. **Number the sentences from 1 to 4 to show the order of events in the creation of Cirque du Soleil.**

   _____ Guy Laliberté gets funding to create a circus.

   _____ Cirque du Soleil has a team of 73 employees.

   _____ A group of artists perform on the streets in Quebec.

   _____ Cirque du Soleil earns more than $1 billion a year.

4. **Which sentence from the passage shows that Guy Laliberté's dream came true?**

   (A) "It all started out as a street show in Quebec, Canada."

   (B) "In the early 1980s, a small group of artists wandered the streets of their small town."

   (C) "All of the details of the show—the music, makeup, dances—are chosen carefully."

   (D) "But over the past 30 years, it has performed in more than 400 cities around the world."

Name: _____   Date: _____

Going Solo in India

1   Picture yourself standing beside one of the biggest rivers in Asia. Can you hear the water roar as it rushes by? Can you feel the spray on your face as the water crashes against large rocks? Now, imagine paddling down this wild river in a small boat. In 2018, Nouria Newman did exactly that. She paddled her kayak more than 230 miles down three of the rivers in Ladakh, India. She was 26 years old—and she did it alone.

2   Nouria Newman was born in France. She started kayaking when she was 5 years old. Now she is one of the best whitewater kayakers in the world. She has won international events and many awards. She has explored rivers all over the world in her kayak. One of her dreams was to kayak on the world-famous rivers of India.

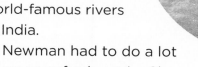

Paddling down a fast-moving river can be very tricky.

3   Newman had to do a lot to prepare for her trip. She studied maps. She had to get permission from the Indian government to travel in Ladakh. She talked to local people for advice. Everything she needed for a week had to fit inside her kayak, so she packed very carefully. She needed warm clothes, safety equipment, camping gear, and food.

4   Some local men drove her to the start of a river called the Zanskar. They left her with her kayak and her gear. The first day of paddling was easy and fairly calm. When it started to get dark and cold, she stopped to make camp. She cooked rice and beans on her small stove and went to sleep. She would be ready for the big rapids to come.

(continued)

5   On the second day, Newman ran into trouble. As she entered a dangerous part of the river, she made a mistake. Her kayak got trapped against a rock, and the river sucked her under. Newman was scared, and no one was there to help. She stayed calm and used her safety training to get out of her kayak. But now she had new problems. She was rushing down a huge river, alone, with no boat.

6   Even though Newman was cold and frightened, she had to keep going. She didn't have another choice. She swam to the side of the river. By an amazing stroke of luck, she managed to grab her kayak and paddle when they floated by. If she had lost her equipment, she would have been stranded in the middle of nowhere. She tried to stay positive and refused to give up. She still had more than 200 miles to go.

Nouria Newman competes in kayaking races, but also paddles for fun.

7   On the third day, Newman saw some local children by the river. They were happy to see her and amazed that she was kayaking alone. Their presence helped her remember why she was there. She loved kayaking and would enjoy this adventure.

8   When Newman woke up on the fifth day, she was ready for the Indus River, one of the largest in the world. Because the snow in the mountains was melting, the river was getting bigger and faster by the hour. Newman was nervous and tired, but she vowed to conquer this river and make no more mistakes.

9   After two more days of wild, rushing water, Newman reached the end of her journey. She had survived and was proud of the challenges she had overcome. But she also learned some hard lessons. She should have been better prepared for danger. Newman plans to keep exploring the world and kayaking. But she's not sure whether she would go on another trip alone. Maybe it's time to share the sport that she loves with others.

Going Solo in India

1. **Which sentences from the passage show that Nouria Newman is a very experienced kayaker? Choose <u>two</u> answers.**

   (A) "In 2018, Nouria Newman did exactly that."

   (B) "She was 26 years old—and she did it alone."

   (C) "She has won international events and many awards."

   (D) "She has explored rivers all over the world in her kayak."

   (E) "One of her dreams was to kayak on the world-famous rivers of India."

2. **What did Newman have to do <u>before</u> she could travel in Ladakh?**

   _____

   _____

3. **How did Newman get into danger on the second day of her trip?**

   (A) Bad weather set in.   (C) A lot of snow melted.

   (B) She made a mistake.   (D) She forgot some gear.

4. **Which sentence from the passage tells why Newman was happy to see children by the river?**

   (A) "If she had lost her equipment, she would have been stranded in the middle of nowhere."

   (B) "She tried to stay positive and refused to give up."

   (C) "They were happy to see her and amazed that she was kayaking alone."

   (D) "Their presence helped her remember why she was there."

5. **Why was the fifth day of Newman's trip so challenging?**

   (A) She got trapped against a rock.

   (B) Her kayak was thrown off course.

   (C) The river was getting bigger and faster.

   (D) She was not prepared for the waterfalls.

Name: _____ Date: _____

8,000 Miles on a Bike With Erik Douds

One of the benefits of biking across the country is seeing the beautiful views.

1   In 2017, Erik Douds rode west across the United States on a road bike. It took him three months to go from New York to California. Then he kept going. He rode north to Canada. He biked the Pacific Coast Trail. He rode to the highest point in North America, which is in Alaska. Even then, he didn't stop. He flew to Asia and rode his bike through India.

2   Douds has biked thousands of miles. He has many stories to tell. Since he is a filmmaker, he creates short films about the people he meets along the way. Douds also has a disease called *diabetes*. But he doesn't let it stop him from doing what he loves.

3   Writer Adele Priestley reached out to Douds, an old schoolmate, for an interview.

PRIESTLEY: Was it always your dream to cycle around the world? How did all this begin?

4   **DOUDS:** I have covered distances that I never could have imagined with just the power of my own two legs. But I actually didn't learn how to ride a bike as a child. In fact, our house had a driveway that was very steep and on top of a hill.

(continued)

Informational Texts for Striving Readers: Grade 5 © 2021 by Michael Priestley, Scholastic Inc. • page 22

That made it hard to learn how to ride. So I found my passion for cycling later in life. A friend invited me to bike across the country. I left my job in New York City. I borrowed a friend's bike. I pretended to know how to use it and learned along the way.

PRIESTLEY: Can you talk a little bit about the challenges of being a long-distance traveler with diabetes?

5   **DOUDS:** I live with a disease called *type 1 diabetes*. Anyone can be diagnosed with it at any point in life. In high school, I suddenly lost a lot of weight. I went to the doctor. That's when I learned about my diagnosis, and my life changed forever.

6   Someone living with any type of diabetes has to be careful to manage their blood-sugar levels. With every meal I have to take a shot of insulin. My body needs that to absorb sugars. The biggest physical challenge I face is passing out from low blood sugar. A special device sends my blood-sugar numbers to a phone every five minutes. How remarkable is that? I use this information to prevent a dangerous situation. Sometimes, I pull over for 15 minutes to eat a snack. That brings my blood sugars back up to normal. I have to carry more snacks than other riders. But just like everyone else, I also have to worry about getting enough water. We all try to keep out of the rain. We have to hide our food from bears. And we try to have fun along the way.

7   I'll tell you that living with a disease for 12 years is a challenge every day. When I first learned about it, I was afraid it would limit my dreams. But here I am, in Bangalore, India. And I'm doing what I love!

PRIESTLEY: What's one piece of advice you would give to someone who wants to go on a really long bike ride?

8   **DOUDS:** Do it! The hardest part of any new journey is the start. Some say that getting out the door is the only thing that matters if you want to go on an adventure. If you want to ride really far, there is only one piece of advice: start pedaling.

PRIESTLEY: Where do you think you'll go next? What are your next goals?

9   **DOUDS:** One of my goals is to bike on every continent. When your entire home fits onto a bike, there is no limit to where you can go next.

8,000 Miles on a Bike With Erik Douds

1. **Why was it hard for Erik Douds to learn how to ride a bike as a child?**

   (A) He had a disease.

   (B) He did not enjoy sports.

   (C) He lived at the top of a steep hill.

   (D) He lived in a city with a lot of traffic.

2. **This question has two parts. Answer Part A. Then answer Part B.**

   PART A

   Based on the interview, which word best describes how Douds felt when he found out he had diabetes?

   (A) angry

   (B) confused

   (C) bored

   (D) worried

   PART B

   Which sentence from the interview best supports the answer to Part A?

   (A) "The biggest physical challenge I face is passing out from low blood sugar."

   (B) "I'll tell you that living with a disease for 12 years is a challenge every day."

   (C) "When I first learned about it, I was afraid it would limit my dreams."

   (D) "But here I am, in Bangalore, India."

3. **How does technology play an important role in Douds's adventures?**

   (A) It helps him manage his diabetes.

   (B) It helps him keep away from bears.

   (C) It helps him stay in touch with friends.

   (D) It helps him track the miles that he rides.

4. **What would Douds most likely tell someone who wants to take a long bike ride?**

   _____

   _____

Name: _____ Date: _____

Make Way for Fun Guy!

1   What is neither a plant nor an animal but is very much alive? *Fungi!* Long ago, scientists used to think fungi (pronounced FUN-jie or FUN-guy) were plants. But plants use the sun, air, and water to make their own food. Fungi can't make their own food. That makes them more like animals. Animals have to find their food. They may eat plants or other animals or both. But unlike animals, fungi can't move around. So scientists decided that fungi belong to their own *kingdom,* or group of living things.

2   Fungi play an **essential** role in helping the earth stay healthy. They often feed on what gets left behind, such as dead plants. As the dead stuff **decays**, fungi turn it into soil. Imagine what would happen if there were no fungi. Dead plants and animals would pile up everywhere!

3   There are different kinds of fungi. Yeast, mold, and mushrooms are just a few examples. They might not seem interesting, but they are very useful. Bakers use yeast to make bread rise. Some kinds of mold are used to make cheese. Others are used to make medicine.

4   Mushrooms are the most familiar type of fungi. They grow in warm, damp places. Some look like small caps on stems. Some are shaped like umbrellas. You've probably eaten mushrooms in salads or soups or sauces. Some mushrooms are so large that people eat them as burgers. In Asia, many people prize a rare kind of mushroom. They pay more than $500 per pound for it. Today, the American **diet** includes more mushrooms than ever. On an **annual** basis, each American eats about four pounds of mushrooms.

5   Some people like to hunt for mushrooms, too. They gather mushrooms in the wild. Some kinds are hard to find, but people love their taste. Experts know which mushrooms to pick and when. But you should never pick mushrooms yourself. Some kinds can make you sick. The bad ones look **similar** to the good ones. So pickers must be careful.

There are different kinds of mushrooms, but they are all fungi.

Make Way for Fun Guy!

1. **What does the word *essential* mean as it is used in paragraph 2?**

   (A) hard to understand

   (B) interesting or amusing

   (C) able to fight disease

   (D) very important or necessary

2. **What is the meaning of the word *decays* in paragraph 2? Write a definition.**

   _____

   _____

3. **Which phrase from paragraph 4 gives a clue to the meaning of *diet*?**

   (A) "so large"

   (B) "more mushrooms"

   (C) "each American eats"

   (D) "four pounds"

4. **What is the meaning of the word *annual* in paragraph 4?**

   (A) per year

   (B) very large

   (C) all at once

   (D) hard to believe

5. **What is the meaning of the word *similar* in the last paragraph? Write a definition.**

   _____

   _____

Name: _____ Date: _____

Crossing the Atlantic

1   Suppose you send a message to your friend in Europe about the latest fad in America. But it takes a few weeks to get there. By the time your friend gets your message, the fad has faded! Back in the 1800s, a letter took weeks or even months to get from America to Europe. Mail traveled by ship across the Atlantic Ocean.

2   A man named Cyrus Field changed all that. With his help, the first transatlantic telegraph cable was laid in 1858. It crossed the Atlantic Ocean from Canada to Ireland. The cable was more than 2,000 miles long. In some places, it was two miles deep under the ocean.

3   With the cable in place, people could send telegrams between the United States and England. The telegrams arrived in minutes! On August 16, 1858, U.S. President James Buchanan **exchanged** messages with Queen Victoria of England.

4   Laying the first cable did not go smoothly, though. Cyrus Field was a **prominent** businessman in New York. He made his fortune selling paper. He knew nothing about the telegraph. But he recognized a chance to make money. He got others to **invest** more than $1 million to pay for the project. Then he asked for navy ships to lay the cable.

Laying of the first trans-Atlantic telegraph cable at Trinity Bay in Newfoundland

5   Attempts to lay the first cable failed twice. Each time, the cable snapped. When the cable finally got connected, it lasted only three weeks. Then the signal died. Field's determination did not **waver**. He raised more money. But then war caused a delay. He had to convince governments to help. He succeeded in the end. A second cable began working in 1866. People on both sides of the ocean were **jubilant**. They celebrated for days, and Cyrus Field became a rich man.

6   Since that time, communications have changed fast. The first radio message crossed the Atlantic in 1927. Telephone cables were laid in the 1930s. Each cable had only one wire. By the 1950s, new cables could handle 36 calls at a time. Today, we have many fiber-optic cables in place. They link all of the continents. They can carry 4 million times the number of voice circuits as the cable of the 1950s. Signals travel around the world at almost the speed of light.

Crossing the Atlantic

1. **What is the meaning of the word *exchanged* in paragraph 3? Write a definition.**

   _____

   _____

2. **What does the word *prominent* mean as it is used in paragraph 4?**
   - (A) very rich
   - (B) clever or skilled
   - (C) well-known or important
   - (D) honest and hard-working

3. **Which phrase from paragraph 4 gives a clue to the meaning of *invest*?**
   - (A) "knew nothing"
   - (B) "a chance"
   - (C) "make money"
   - (D) "pay for the project"

4. **What is the meaning of the word *waver* in paragraph 5? Write a definition.**

   _____

   _____

5. **Which phrase in paragraph 5 gives a clue to the meaning of *jubilant*?**
   - (A) "caused a delay"
   - (B) "succeeded in the end"
   - (C) "both sides of the ocean"
   - (D) "celebrated for days"

Name: _____   Date: _____

Augusta Savage, Artist Extraordinaire

1   *The Pugilist* is a famous sculpture created in 1942. The name means "fighter." It is a sculpture of boxer Jack Johnson, who became the world's first Black heavyweight champion in 1908. It shows him with his arms folded. He looks up with confidence, ready to face anything.

2   That fighting spirit was a reflection of its sculptor, Augusta Savage. Augusta was born in Green Cove Springs, Florida, in 1892. As a child, she liked to make small figures. She used the red clay near her home. That was the start of her life's work as a sculptor. Her father did not want her to be an artist. But she **persisted**, in spite of the many challenges she faced.

The Harp, by Augusta Savage, was featured at the 1939 World's Fair.

3   As an adult, Savage moved to West Palm Beach. There, she **pursued** her career as an artist and won some prizes. But Savage could not sell her artwork in Florida. So she moved to New York City to study art. She **enrolled** in an art course at Cooper Union in 1921. Over the next few years, she became an **influential** artist. Her work had an effect on many others in the Harlem Renaissance. That was a movement of Black writers and artists in the 1920s and 30s.

(continued)

4   Savage made a number of sculptures in the 1920s. Some were busts of famous people, such as W.E.B. DuBois. In 1929, she created one of her finest works. It was a sculpture of a boy called *Gamin*. That helped earn enough money to pay for her to travel and study **abroad**. She spent the next three years working in Europe. When she returned to New York, she opened a workshop and began teaching other Black artists.

5   In later years, Savage became known for her other works. One, *The Harp*, appeared at the 1939 World's Fair in New York City. It showed a choir of singing Black children. Savage was the only Black woman to get a commission at the fair. Unfortunately, many of her works, including *The Harp*, no longer exist. But her legacy lives on in her students, some of whom became famous themselves.

1. **What does the word *persisted* mean in paragraph 2?**

    (A) ran away   (C) grew quickly

    (B) kept trying   (D) did not agree

2. **What does the word *pursued* mean as it is used in paragraph 3?**

    (A) completed   (C) worked toward

    (B) earned money   (D) took a break from

3. **In paragraph 3, what is the meaning of *enrolled*?**

    (A) signed up   (C) studied hard

    (B) created art   (D) paid the cost

4. **Which phrase in paragraph 3 gives a clue to the meaning of *influential*?**

    (A) "sell her artwork"   (C) "had an effect on"

    (B) "Over the next few years" (D) "a movement"

5. **What is the meaning of the word *abroad* in paragraph 4? Write a definition.**

    _____

    _____

Informational Texts for Striving Readers: Grade 5 • © 2021 by Michael Priestley, Scholastic Inc. • page 30

Name: _____ Date: _____

The First Diving Machine

Informational Texts for Striving Readers: Grade 5 © 2021 by Michael Priestley, Scholastic Inc. • page 31

1   For many years, John Lethbridge wondered what lay under the sea. He wanted to explore the ocean, but he had no way to do it. So he invented the world's first diving machine. It allowed him to go underwater to see what was there.

2   Born in 1675, Lethbridge lived in Newton Abbot, a town in England. In his day job, he sold wool at the town market. No one really knows what made him want to dive in the ocean. Maybe he needed a way to make more money for his family. He had 17 children to feed. But, for whatever reason, he built a kind of diving suit in 1715.

3   Lethbridge called his invention "The Diving Machine." It was a wooden barrel about six feet long. It had a round window and two holes for the arms. Lethbridge laid on his stomach inside the barrel. He put his arms through the holes. He could look through the window to see what was below him. The arm holes had leather seals to keep water out.

An artist's drawing of Lethbridge's "Diving Machine"

4   With this suit, Lethbridge could go underwater to about 50 feet. Below that, the barrel started to leak. With only the air inside the barrel, he could breathe for about 30 minutes. Helpers used cables to lower the machine into the water and raise it back up. Lethbridge sent signals with ropes that he could pull.

5   Lethbridge began using his machine to explore shipwreck sites. He hoped to find sunken treasure—and he did. Soon, companies who had lost ships heard about him. They hired him to find their lost cargo.

(continued)

6   One wreck was the *Slotter Hooge*, a Dutch ship. It sank off the coast of Portugal in 1724. It contained three tons of silver. It also held chests full of coins. The Dutch East India Company hired Lethbridge to recover the lost loot. Using his machine, he made several dives that year. He brought up more than half of the silver and coins from the sunken ship. The company paid him a lot of money to do it.

7   Over the next 30 years, Lethbridge made many more dives. He found lost cargo. He also recovered lots of treasure. He became very rich.

8   His original machine did not last. But he made drawings of it. From those drawings, other people built models. They hang in museums in several parts of the world. One hangs at Newton Abbot, where it all began.

1. **How does the author present information in the first paragraph of this passage?**
   (A) by explaining causes and effects
   (B) by describing events in time order
   (C) by comparing and contrasting events
   (D) by describing a problem and its solution

2. **This question has two parts. Answer Part A. Then answer Part B.**

   PART A
   What text structure does the author use in the rest of the passage?
   (A) time order
   (B) cause and effect
   (C) problem and solution
   (D) comparison and contrast

   PART B
   Which sentences from the passage support the answer to Part A? Choose <u>two</u> answers.
   (A) "In his day job, he sold wool at the town market."
   (B) "But, for whatever reason, he built a kind of diving suit in 1715."
   (C) "With this suit, Lethbridge could go underwater to about 50 feet."
   (D) "Below that, the barrel started to leak."
   (E) "It sank off the coast of Portugal in 1724."

Name: _____   Date: _____

Fighting With Respect

1   What do you think of when you hear the term *martial arts?* If you say "fighting," you're not alone. The word *martial* refers to war or fighting. But martial arts involve much more.

2   There are at least 170 different forms of martial arts. They include sumo wrestling and judo. All of them combine movement, self-defense, and mental training. Students take part in matches to show their skills. Each martial art has its own history and rules. But many of them share certain features. Three very popular forms are *karate*, *muay thai*, and *capoeira*.

3   Karate came from Japan with a strong influence from China. The word *karate* means "empty hand." People do not use any weapons. They use only their hands and feet.

Before fighting, opponents bow to each other to show respect.

4   Physical training is central to karate. But so are respect, honesty, and non-violence. These are important ideas. Students learn to respect their teacher. They also respect themselves and their opponent. Grace, good form, and a calm mind are just as important as strength and power.

5   Like many other martial arts, karate has different levels of skill. For each level, there is a different-colored belt. Students wear the belt with a uniform called a *gi*. It is a loose two-piece outfit, usually white. It has a jacket and pants.

6   Another well-known martial art is muay thai (pronounced MOY tie). It comes from Thailand. Like karate, it had some influence from China. And, as in karate, fighters use their hands and feet. But muay thai also allows the use of elbows and knees. Training for this sport builds power, speed, and fitness.

7   The traditions of muay thai have been passed down for hundreds of years. Being a muay thai fighter is not just a sport; it is a way of life. Fighters start training when they are very young. They must show respect to their teacher before they can enter the gym. They only begin fighting when their teacher says they are ready. Fighters often earn money to support their families. And they are honored with festivals, music, and dancing.

(continued)

8   Like karate, muay thai is an Olympic sport. But safety is very important. Fighters must wear safety gear so they don't hurt each other. Gear includes head and mouth guards, pads, and gloves. Muay thai does not have belts to show levels of skill, as karate does. There is no uniform, either. Most fighters wear only loose shorts and perhaps a shirt.

9   Capoeira (kap-uh-WEH-ra) is a third kind of martial art. Unlike karate and muay thai, it does not come from Asia. It is from Brazil, but it comes from West African culture. Enslaved African people in Brazil were not allowed to fight. So they hid their kicks and punches in a dance. They mixed the movements with music.

Some people think that breakdancing came from capoeira.

10   Capoeira is a performance as well as a martial art. People wear loose-fitting shirts and pants, usually white. Many schools use colored belts or cords to show skill levels. Some performances offer only dances. They show off skillful moves and tumbles. In others, people compete to make their opponent lose rhythm or fall over.

11   Most martial arts come from very old traditions. They combine both mental and physical elements. They also teach about respect, discipline, and culture.

Fighting With Respect

1. **This question has two parts. Answer Part A. Then answer Part B.**

   PART A

   What structure does the author use to organize information in this passage?

   (A) time order

   (B) cause and effect

   (C) problem and solution

   (D) comparison and contrast

   PART B

   Which sentence from the passage best supports the answer to Part A?

   (A) "The word *martial* refers to war or fighting."

   (B) "There are at least 170 different forms of martial arts."

   (C) "For each level, there is a different-colored belt."

   (D) "Like karate, it had some influence from China."

2. **What is one <u>difference</u> between karate and muay thai?**

   (A) Karate doesn't allow kicks, but muay thai does.

   (B) Karate is an Olympic sport, but muay thai is not.

   (C) Karate has a traditional uniform, but muay thai does not.

   (D) Karate uses weapons, but muay thai uses only the body.

3. **How is capoeira <u>different</u> from both karate and muay thai?**

   (A) It is not from Asia.

   (B) It has a long history.

   (C) It is an Olympic sport.

   (D) It does not allow competition.

4. **Read the descriptions in the chart. Check the box or boxes beside each description to tell if it fits karate, muay thai, and/or capoeira.**

Descriptions	Karate	Muay Thai	Capoeira
Students usually wear white clothing.			
It uses protective gear in the Olympics.			
Respect is very important.			
Colored belts show skill levels.			

Name: _____   Date: _____

The Toughest Horse Race in the World

Small but sturdy, Mongolian horses have hardly changed in hundreds of years.

1   The world's longest, toughest horse race happens every year in the Asian country of Mongolia. But the idea behind it started more than 800 years ago. Back in 1224, ruler Genghis Khan started a mail system. Men on horseback carried messages and letters across the Mongolian Empire. Riders traveled as fast as they could. They stopped often at stations along the way to change horses. In this way, riders could cover as many as 200 miles a day. Messages could be sent 4,000 miles in just a few weeks.

2   With a nod to that long-ago mail route, the Mongol Derby began in 2009. The goal is to ride 1,000 kilometers (about 620 miles) on horseback in just 10 days. The course follows parts of the route that the mail riders used. Each year, about 45 men and women enter the race. They come from many countries. About half of the riders drop out before they reach the finish.

3   Mongolia lies between China and Russia. It is known for its wild landscapes. During the Mongol Derby, riders cross open plains, wide rivers, and deep valleys. They climb high mountain passes. They ride through wetlands and deserts. The temperature changes are extreme.

(continued)

4   Riders try to cover 75 to 100 miles each day. But they must change horses every 25 miles or so. The race requires more than 1,000 horses for all the riders. Horses wait at stations along the route. Making sure the horses stay healthy and safe is an important part of the race. At each station, riders must have their horses checked by a vet before getting new ones. If a horse is injured or too tired, then the rider gets penalized.

5   The Mongolian horses used in the Derby are like those used on the mail route in the 1200s. They are small but very tough and have short, strong legs. They can survive in rough conditions. Most of the horses are half wild. Riding so many different, half-trained horses can be hard. Even the best riders fall off a few times during the race. They have to be careful not to get injured.

6   Racers can only ride during the day. By 8:00 P.M., they must stop and find a place to stay. Some sleep outside. Others stay in local homes. The course itself is not marked, so riders have to find their own way. Using maps, a GPS, and instinct, they ride through rain, wind, storms, cold, and heat.

7   In 2013, a British writer named Lara Prior-Palmer became the first woman to win the Derby. At age 19, she was also the youngest winner. On the first day, she got lost and her horse got injured. She had to walk beside her horse in the heat for many miles. She almost quit on the first day, but she kept going. By the end of the race, Prior-Palmer was completely exhausted. Her whole body hurt, and her ankles and knees were swollen. But she finished the race in 6 days and 8 hours. A few years later, she wrote a book about the experience.

8   In 2019, 70-year-old American Bob Long became the oldest person to win the Mongol Derby. He had been riding horses his whole life and was well prepared. Long rode so fast that he stayed a few hours ahead of the group for most of the race. Finding the way by himself was scary, and there were times when he wanted to give up. By the end, Long was happy just to finish the race. Coming in first was an added bonus.

9   Every year in August, new riders trek to Mongolia for the Derby. Each Derby runs on a slightly different course, and each year the riders face many challenges. We can only wait and see who will make history next at the toughest horse race in the world.

MONGOLIA

The Toughest Horse Race in the World

1. **This question has two parts. Answer Part A. Then answer Part B.**

    PART A **How does the author organize most of the information in this passage?**

    (A) by comparing and contrasting

    (B) by explaining causes and effects

    (C) by describing a problem and its solution

    (D) by telling about events in chronological order

    PART B **Which two sentences support the answer to Part A?**

    (A) "Messages could be sent 4,000 miles in just a few weeks."

    (B) "With a nod to that long-ago mail route, the Mongol Derby began in 2009."

    (C) "Making sure the horses stay healthy and safe is an important part of the race."

    (D) "The Mongolian horses used in the Derby are like those used on the mail route in the 1200s."

    (E) "In 2013, a British writer named Lara Prior-Palmer became the first woman to win the Derby."

2. **How is the Mongol Derby similar to Genghis Khan's mail system?**

    (A) It has many horse stations.   (C) It allows only male riders.

    (B) It is very expensive.   (D) It takes weeks to complete.

3. **Which sentence from the passage best explains why riding across Mongolia is so challenging?**

    (A) "Each year, about 45 men and women enter the race."

    (B) "Mongolia lies between China and Russia."

    (C) "It is known for its wild landscapes."

    (D) "Racers can only ride during the day."

4. **Which sentence in paragraph 6 uses a cause-effect structure? Underline the sentence.**

    Racers can only ride during the day. By 8:00 P.M., they must stop and find a place to stay. Some sleep outside. Others stay in local homes. The course itself is not marked, so riders have to find their own way. Using maps, a GPS, and instinct, they ride through rain, wind, storms, cold, and heat.

Informational Texts for Striving Readers: Grade 5 © 2021 by Michael Priestley, Scholastic Inc. • page 38

Name: _____ Date: _____

Grandma Moses

Grandma Moses liked to paint simple scenes of American rural life.

1   Did you know that one of the most famous American artists didn't begin painting until age 78? Grandma Moses's paintings have appeared in museums and art shows all over the world. They have been used for greeting cards and posters, even a postage stamp. She was a remarkable artist and one of the best-loved people in America.

2   Anna Mary Robertson was born in 1860 in upstate New York. Growing up on a farm, she worked hard. She churned butter and baked bread. She made pickles and sewed clothing. She did needlework and boiled maple syrup. For fun, she drew pictures of things on the farm. Like many farm girls then, she spent little time in school.

3   In 1887, Robertson married Thomas Moses. They worked on a farm in Virginia and raised five children. They moved back to New York in 1905. When her husband died in 1927, Grandma Moses kept the farm going for a while. Then she began to paint. Many of her simple pictures showed farm scenes, such as apple picking. One was titled *Catching the Thanksgiving Turkey*. Another was called *Over the River to Grandma's House*.

4   In 1939, an art dealer saw some of Moses's works. They were hanging in a drugstore in Hoosick Falls, New York. He bought ten of them. He showed them to art collectors and made Moses famous. Later that year, some of her paintings hung at the Museum of Modern Art in New York. In all, she painted more than 2,000 works of art and had more than 250 art shows.

(continued)

5   Grandma Moses became known as a "naive" artist. She didn't have any formal training as an artist. Her school of art became known as "American Primitive." She painted simple pictures that looked like real life. She used lively colors and showed everyday things.

6   Many people loved Moses's work. Maybe it reminded them of their own childhood. Others thought her work looked like something a child might do. But when she died in 1961 at age 101, the whole country felt sad. President John F. Kennedy said, "Her passing takes away a beloved figure from American life. . . . All Americans mourn her loss."

---

1. **Why did the author write this passage?**

   (A) to describe what life on a farm was like

   (B) to tell about the life and work of Grandma Moses

   (C) to explain how a farm girl taught herself to paint

   (D) to compare Grandma Moses's works to other artists

2. **Which sentence from the first paragraph gives the author's view of Grandma Moses? Underline the sentence.**

   Did you know that one of the most famous American artists didn't begin painting until age 78? Grandma Moses's paintings have appeared in museums and art shows all over the world. They have been used for greeting cards and posters, even a postage stamp. She was a remarkable artist and one of the best-loved people in America.

3. **Which details from the passage tell what people thought of Grandma Moses's artwork? Choose two answers.**

   (A) "In 1939, an art dealer saw some of Moses's works. They were hanging in a drugstore in Hoosick Falls, New York."

   (B) "She painted simple pictures that looked like real life."

   (C) "Many people loved Moses's work. Maybe it reminded them of their own childhood."

   (D) "Others thought her work looked like something a child might do."

   (E) "'Her passing takes away a beloved figure from American life.'"

Name: _____ Date: _____

Read both texts about a volcanic eruption in Chile. Then answer the questions.

TEXT A

Calbuco Volcano Erupts

1   On April 22, 2015, Calbuco erupted without warning. Calbuco Volcano is located in Ensenada, a small town in southern Chile. The volcano had been quiet since 1972. At 6:04 P.M., the volcano suddenly began to spew hardened pieces of lava, ash, and hot gases into the air. The eruption lasted 90 minutes. The ash cloud above the volcano was 50,000 feet high. Everyone living around the volcano had to evacuate immediately. No injuries were reported.

TEXT B

A View of Calbuco
by Pablo Saumann (a first-hand account)

2   That morning of April 22, I woke up expecting a normal day. The weather was beautiful and sunny. I ate breakfast and looked out the window at Calbuco, as I did every morning. My dogs were running through the trees. The view of the green forest and snow-capped volcano took my breath away. I smiled at the paradise in my backyard.

Calbuco volcano in southern Chile

3   I spent most of the day working in the garden. Then I fed my chickens and threw sticks for the dogs. Late in the afternoon, I decided to go to the store. So I put the dogs in the house, locked the door, and drove to town.

4   I was just leaving the store when I felt the ground shake. Nobody else seemed to notice. I thought that maybe I had imagined it. But then the ground shook again. Suddenly, with a huge rumble, the top of Calbuco exploded into the air.

(continued)

5   Ash, rocks, and chunks of hard lava flew high into the air. It made a tower so high that I couldn't see the top. All around me, people ran out of houses and stores. We all stood on the road, looking up into the sky. Nobody had imagined that Calbuco would erupt like this.

A large cloud of ash erupts out of Calbuco volcano.

6   Then small volcanic rocks and ash started to rain down around us. Suddenly, an emergency siren started to sound. It was very loud. I realized that everyone needed to get out of town quickly. I got into my car and drove to Puerto Varas, a nearby city. The police directed everyone to safe places indoors. From my safe shelter, I watched the tower of ash begin to collapse around the volcano. As the sun was setting, the sky turned pink and orange. It was a beautiful and scary thing to see.

7   All of us had to stay in the city for a few days. Nobody got hurt. We were lucky that we all got out of the town quickly. But we were worried about our homes and farms, and I worried about my dogs. I didn't know if my house would still be standing.

8   Finally, it was safe for us to go home. My road was buried in ash about a meter deep, so I had to hike the last few miles. When I arrived, I was amazed to see most of my house still standing. Only one corner of the roof had fallen in. Unbelievably, my dogs had also survived. They must have jumped out through a broken window, but they were very hungry and thirsty. I hugged my dogs and cried with happiness.

9   Ensenada looked like a new planet. Everything was covered in volcanic material, mostly ash. There was no more grass. All of the trees had lost their leaves. The rivers were gone, and there were no animals in sight. The land looked lifeless. I felt like I was on the moon.

10   It took us a few years to rebuild Ensenada. The townspeople slowly started to clear out the ash, dig out buried cars, and fix our houses. We planted new grass. The leaves grew back on the trees.

(continued)

Informational Texts for Striving Readers: Grade 5 © 2021 by Michael Priestley, Scholastic Inc. • page 42

11   I'm back in my home. I wake up each morning and look out the window at Calbuco. The volcano is quiet—for now. I take care of my dogs and work in the garden. This is my home. I still love my backyard paradise, and the view still takes my breath away. It reminds me that I'm lucky to be alive.

1. **What is the main purpose of Text A?**

   (A) to explain why a volcano erupted

   (B) to convince people to move away

   (C) to report the facts about Calbuco

   (D) to describe the people of Ensenada

2. **According to both texts, what happened just after the eruption began?**

   (A) The townspeople evacuated.

   (B) All of the roads were closed.

   (C) The corner of a house fell in.

   (D) All of the dogs started barking.

3. **How is Text B different from Text A? Choose two answers.**

   (A) It describes Ensenada.

   (B) It is written in first person.

   (C) It gives the date of April 22.

   (D) It says that no one got hurt.

   (E) It expresses personal feelings.

4. **Which sentence tells how Pablo Saumann felt when he first returned to his home after the eruption?**

   (A) "Finally, it was safe for us to go home."

   (B) "My road was buried in ash about a meter deep, so I had to hike the last few miles."

   (C) "When I arrived, I was amazed to see most of my house still standing."

   (D) "Everything was covered in volcanic material, mostly ash."

5. **Based on Text B, why did Saumann stay in Ensenada even after the eruption?**

   (A) He loved the natural beauty of his home.

   (B) He didn't think the volcano would erupt again.

   (C) He didn't want to leave his friends and family.

   (D) He enjoyed the excitement of living in danger.

Name: _____ Date: _____

Read both texts about the stone statues on Rapa Nui. Then answer the questions.

TEXT A

Rapa Nui

Moai, **large stone statues, stand along the coast of Rapa Nui.**

1   About 2,200 miles west of Chile lies an island called Rapa Nui. Its English name is Easter Island. It is 14 miles long and 7 miles wide. Its nearest neighbor is 1,100 miles away. On the island, visitors may see a line of large stone statues. These are the *moai.* To see them gives one a sense of awe. No one knows exactly why they were built or what they mean. But they have stood in place for hundreds of years.

2   People from a Pacific island far to the west landed on Rapa Nui around 700 CE. When they got there, palm trees and plants covered the land. The people settled on the island and built homes. About 500 years later, they began to create the moai. The people carved more than 900 of them. They used a kind of volcanic rock called *tuff.* Almost all of the statues came from one quarry. Then they were moved to other parts of the island. Most of them stand about 13 feet high and weigh about 14 tons. A few are much larger. Each statue sits on a stone base called an *ahu.*

(continued)

3   Many experts have tried to figure out how the people moved the moai to places miles away. An old myth claims that the statues "walked" to their new homes. But that word may just describe how they were moved. Experts also wonder about their purpose. Some of the statues held burial rooms at one time. So they might stand for leaders who died. But no one really knows.

4   A Dutch explorer found Rapa Nui in 1722. He landed on Easter Sunday and named the island for that day. At the time, about 3,000 people lived there. But it had almost no trees and no crops. Over the next 150 years, the island saw civil war, smallpox, and farming problems. The number of people went down to about 110. In 1888, Chile took over the island and used most of it for sheep farming. In 1965, people on the island became citizens of Chile.

TEXT B
A Mystery Solved

5   For about 30 years, scientists studied the moai on Easter Island. They wanted to find the meaning of the stone statues. In 2019, they found an answer.

6   First, the researchers made a map of where the moai were set. From the map, they noted that the moai stood in places that had fresh water. Then they tested the soil in the quarry where the moai were made. They found traces of food crops, such as bananas and sweet potatoes. This clue suggested that the stone in the quarry held nutrients needed to grow crops. Researchers think the people placed the statues in certain spots near fresh water. This way, they honored the soil and helped it produce food.

7   This theory helps explain how the people lived on Rapa Nui long ago. The soil was rich, and they grew their own food. But over many decades, the people foolishly cut down all of the trees on the island. That caused the soil to erode and wash away. Today, the soil is rocky and bare. It does not support farming. Perhaps that is why it took so long to figure out that the moai were connected to crops.

The moai are made of volcanic rock.

Rapa Nui

1. **What is the main purpose of Text A?**

    (A) to tell how Rapa Nui was formed

    (B) to convince people to visit Rapa Nui

    (C) to explain how the moai were carved

    (D) to describe the stone statues of Rapa Nui

2. **Which sentence in the first paragraph gives the author's view of the moai? Underline the sentence.**

    About 2,200 miles west of Chile lies an island called Rapa Nui. Its English name is Easter Island. It is 14 miles long and 7 miles wide. Its nearest neighbor is 1,100 miles away. On the island, visitors may see a line of large stone statues. These are the *moai*. To see them gives one a sense of awe. No one knows exactly why they were built or what they mean. But they have stood in place for hundreds of years.

3. **What is the purpose of Text B?**

    (A) to explain a theory about what the stone statues mean

    (B) to compare the past and present on Rapa Nui

    (C) to tell how the people of Rapa Nui grew crops

    (D) to describe the scientists who studied the moai

4. **In the last paragraph of Text B, which sentence contains an opinion? Underline the sentence.**

    This theory helps explain how the people lived on Rapa Nui long ago. The soil was rich, and they grew their own food. But over many decades, the people foolishly cut down all of the trees on the island. That caused the soil to erode and wash away. Today, the soil is rocky and bare. It does not support farming. Perhaps that is why it took so long to figure out that the moai were connected to crops.

5. **Based on Text B, why did the people of Rapa Nui carve the stone statues?**

    (A) to scare away visitors to the island

    (B) to keep the soil from washing away

    (C) to honor the soil and help grow crops

    (D) to remember important people who died

Informational Texts for Striving Readers: Grade 5 © 2021 by Michael Priestley, Scholastic Inc. • page 46

Name: _____ Date: _____

Remembering the *Hindenburg*

1   Can you imagine a time when people did not travel by airplane? Believe it or not, that was only a hundred years ago. Back then, people crossed the ocean by ship. The trip from Europe to the United States could take weeks. Then, in the 1930s, a new way of travel began. People started flying by *airship*, or blimp. These airships were also called *zeppelins* after a German general who built them.

2   An airship was basically a huge tube filled with a gas, usually helium. The gas was lighter than air, so the airship rose. Below the tube was a cabin. The air crew and passengers rode in the cabin. Airships could take people from Europe to the U.S. in a few days. People could eat, sleep, and enjoy themselves in the airship cabin. It was a nice way to travel.

The *Hindenburg* next to its hangar in Germany

3   One of the greatest airships was called the *Hindenburg*. On May 3, 1937, it left Germany on its 63rd flight. It was headed to the United States. Unfortunately, it was filled with hydrogen, an unsafe gas. On board were 36 passengers and 61 crew members. The weather in the U.S. was not very good when the *Hindenburg* arrived. The pilot had to delay the landing. He circled over New York City until he got the okay to land.

4   When the airship finally began to descend, the pilot had to release some of the gas in the tube to keep the airship level. As the airship connected to the landing tower, there was a spark. No one can say for sure what caused the spark. But the spark hit the gas, and the gas exploded. The airship blew up. Of the 97 people on board, 62 survived; 35 did not. It was a terrible disaster.

(continued)

5   Hundreds of people were waiting for the *Hindenburg* to arrive. They watched the explosion happen, but only one of them got hurt. That was the last airship flight to the United States. The age of airships came to an end. Soon afterward, airplanes took over. They were much safer.

The *Hindenburg's* Timeline

MAY 3, 1937

7:16 P.M.   Leaves Frankfurt, Germany

MAY 4

2:00 A.M.   Begins crossing Atlantic Ocean

MAY 6

12:00 P.M. Reaches Boston

3:00 P.M.   Flies over New York City

4:15 P.M.   Reaches Lakehurst, New Jersey

7:21 P.M.   Drops landing ropes at Lakehurst

7:25 P.M.   *Hindenburg* bursts into flames

The Flight of the *Hindenburg*

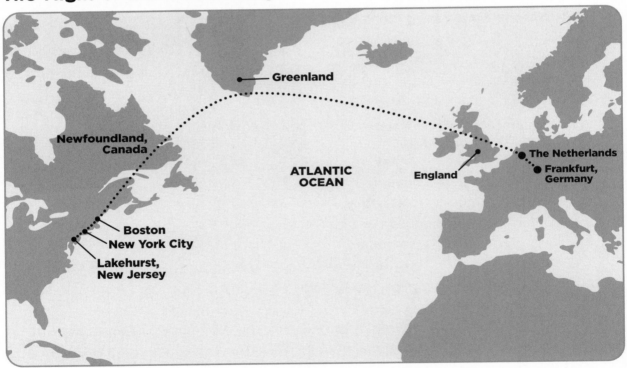

Remembering the *Hindenburg*

1. **About how long did the *Hindenburg* take to fly from Germany to the United States?**

   _____

2. **What island did the *Hindenburg* pass halfway through its flight to the United States?**

   _____

3. **In what city did the *Hindenburg* land?**

   A Frankfurt   **C** New York City
   B Boston   **D** Lakehurst

4. **This question has two parts. Answer Part A. Then answer Part B.**

   PART A

   Why did the *Hindenburg* circle over New York City on May 6?

   A It was low on fuel.   **C** The pilot could not see the airport.
   B Its landing was delayed.   **D** Passengers wanted to see the city.

   PART B

   Which sentence from the passage supports the answer to Part A?

   A "On May 3, 1937, it left Germany on its 63rd flight."

   B "On board were 36 passengers and 61 crew members."

   C "The weather in the U.S. was not very good when the *Hindenburg* arrived."

   D "When the airship finally began to descend, the pilot had to release some of the gas in the tube to keep the airship level."

5. **Which sentence in the last paragraph best tells what happened as a result of the *Hindenburg* disaster? Underline the sentence.**

   Hundreds of people were waiting for the *Hindenburg* to arrive. They watched the explosion happen, but only one of them got hurt. That was the last airship flight to the United States. The age of airships came to an end. Soon afterward, airplanes took over. They were much safer.

Name: _____ Date: _____

The Bees of Notre-Dame

1   When fire nearly destroyed the Notre-Dame de Paris in 2019, people around the world were stunned. Many think it is the greatest cathedral in the world. It is surely the most famous. People watched and waited anxiously for hours. They feared that the huge church would not survive the fire. Other people also worried about some of the residents at Notre-Dame. It is home to 80,000 bees.

2   In 2013, the city of Paris, France, decided to help nature by raising bees. The government put more than 700 beehives in places all over the city. Three were placed on the roof of Notre-Dame. Those three hives support many thousands of bees. They produce 165 pounds of honey every year.

3   Beekeeper Nicolas Geant takes care of the bees at Notre-Dame. After watching the wooden roof of the church collapse, he was worried. Then the huge *spire*, or steeple, fell. He didn't know if the bees could live through the fire.

4   When firefighters at last put out the fire, Geant checked the hives on the stone roof near the back of the church. He was thrilled to see bees buzzing in and out of the hives once again. Smoke from the fire must have put the bees to sleep. They stayed in their hives until the fire went out. Beekeepers often use smoke to keep bees calm as they work around the hives. Smoke does not hurt the bees. And in this case, it may have saved them.

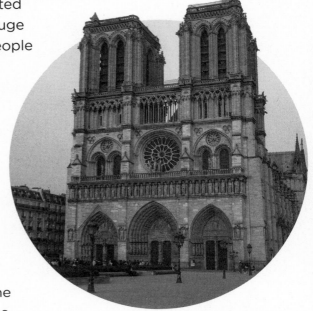

Notre-Dame cathedral
before the fire

Notre-Dame Facts

When the church was built, it was the tallest building in Europe.

Dates of Construction: begun 1163, completed about 1270

Age: more than 850 years

Number of Visitors per Year: 12 million

Height of Spire: 315 feet (96 meters)

Weight of Spire: 750 tons

Height of Ceiling: 108 feet (33 meters)

The Bees of Notre-Dame

1. **What was special about Notre-Dame when it was built?**
    (A) It was all made of stone.
    (B) It had beehives on the roof.
    (C) It had stained-glass windows.
    (D) It was the tallest building in Europe.

2. **About how many people visit Notre-Dame each year?**

    _____

3. **Which <u>two</u> sentences in the last paragraph explain how the bees survived the fire? Underline the sentences.**

    When firefighters at last put out the fire, Geant checked the hives on the stone roof near the back of the church. He was thrilled to see bees buzzing in and out of the hives once again. Smoke from the fire must have put the bees to sleep. They stayed in their hives until the fire went out. Beekeepers often use smoke to keep bees calm as they work around the hives. Smoke does not hurt the bees. And in this case, it may have saved them.

4. **About how long did it take to build Notre-Dame?**

    _____

5. **Which sentence from the passage tells why bees were living at Notre-Dame?**
    (A) "It is home to 80,000 bees."
    (B) "The government put more than 700 beehives in places all over the city."
    (C) "They produce 165 pounds of honey every year."
    (D) "Beekeeper Nicolas Geant takes care of the bees at Notre-Dame."

Name: _____   Date: _____

A Language of Hope

1   What if all the people in the world spoke the same language? Would we get along with one another better? That's what Dr. Ludwig Zamenhof thought.

2   Zamenhof lived in Poland in the city of Bialystok. He was born in 1859 and grew up to become an eye doctor. In the late 1800s, Poles, Russians, Jews, Lithuanians, and Germans all lived in his city. They spoke many languages and did not always get along. Dr. Zamenhof thought they might be more likely to see eye to eye if they could all understand one another. So he made up a language they could all learn. He called it "The International Language." As the creator, he called himself Doktoro Esperanto. Before long, the language itself became known as Esperanto. The name means "the hoping one."

Dr. Ludwig Zamenhof, creator of Esperanto

3   Zamenhof wrote his first book on Esperanto in 1887. It contained 920 word roots and a list of affixes. These roots and affixes could be used to form thousands of words. For example, *lerni* means "learn." The word *lernejo* means "school," and *lernanto* means "student."

4   The book also featured a basic alphabet and 16 rules of grammar. The alphabet had a total of 34 sounds. They were represented by letters or letter pairs. Everything about the language was meant to be easy to understand. For example, every word was spelled as it sounded. All verbs were regular and had only one form for each tense. Every noun ended in *-o*, as in *amiko*, which means "friend." Every adjective ended in *-a*, as in *bona*, which means "good." An ending could be added for a plural.

5   Dr. Zamenhof dreamed that people all over the world would learn his new language. Then everyone would be able to communicate. A meeting of people from many countries took place in France in 1905. The goal was to talk about the language and how to spread its use. The language itself was based mainly on European languages. So it was fairly easy for Europeans to learn. It was not that easy for people in other language groups, such as those in Asia and Africa.

(continued)

Informational Texts for Striving Readers: Grade 5 © 2021 by Michael Priestley, Scholastic Inc. • page 52

6   The effort to spread the use of Esperanto made some progress. A group of Esperanto speakers founded the Universal Esperanto Association in 1908. Over the years, it gained members in 83 countries. It has published more than 30,000 books and 100 magazines in Esperanto. Some radio stations broadcast news in Esperanto. Some professional groups use it for communication.

Could a universal language make people from different parts of the world get along better?

7   But the number of people who can speak or write Esperanto has never reached the peak that Dr. Zamenhof hoped for. Some sources claim that about 2 million people speak Esperanto today. Other sources say the number is closer to 100,000. That is a very small part of the world's population.

When Dr. Zamenhof invented Esperanto, the world had less than 2 billion people. Today, that number is about 8 billion. We speak hundreds of different languages. And—as in 1887—we do not always get along. The ten most widely used languages in the world are spoken by only about 3.6 billion people, or less than half the total population. One could argue that the need for an international language has never been greater.

TOP TEN LANGUAGES

Language*	First-Language Speakers (in millions)
Chinese	1,310
Spanish	460
English	379
Hindi	341
Arabic	319
Bengali	228
Portuguese	220
Russian	154
Japanese	128
Lahnda (Punjabi)	119

Source: *The World Almanac and Book of Facts 2020* (*Note: Some of these languages, such as Chinese and Lahnda, include several dialects.)

A Language of Hope

1. **What made Dr. Zamenhof want to invent a new language?**

   (A) He was an eye doctor.

   (B) He grew up in Poland.

   (C) His city had many ethnic groups who did not get along.

   (D) His city did not have good schools.

2. **What made Esperanto simple and easy for everyone to learn? Choose two answers.**

   (A) It had 920 word roots.

   (B) All verbs were regular.

   (C) People in different places could understand it.

   (D) Every word was spelled as it was pronounced.

   (E) The alphabet had 34 sounds represented by letters.

3. **Which sentence in the paragraph 5 best explains why people in China or Egypt might have difficulty learning Esperanto? Underline the sentence.**

   Dr. Zamenhof dreamed that people all over the world would learn his new language. Then everyone would be able to communicate. A meeting of people from many countries took place in France in 1905. The goal was to talk about the language and how to spread its use. The language itself was based mainly on European languages. So it was fairly easy for Europeans to learn. It was not that easy for people in other language groups, such as those in Asia and Africa.

4. **About how many people can speak or write Esperanto today?**

   _____

5. **After Chinese, what is the most widely spoken language in the world?**

   _____

6. **About how many people speak English as their first language?**

   (A) 119 million

   (B) 379 million

   (C) 460 million

   (D) 3.6 billion

Name: _____   Date: _____

Got Bugs?

1   Care to snack on some delicious bugs? Some people say grasshoppers have a nutty taste. Ants taste a little sweet. Stinkbugs taste like apples. Perhaps you have tried some of these treats for yourself?

2   Not long ago, the United Nations (UN) issued a report on world hunger. The number of people on Earth keeps growing. In the future, we may not be able to grow enough food to feed everyone. Looking ahead, the UN says that we should eat more bugs. Since there are at least 2,000 types of edible insects, we should have plenty to choose from.

This dish of crispy wood worms is rich in protein.

3   More than 2 billion people in more than 100 countries already eat bugs. The most widely eaten kinds are beetles, moths, bees, ants, and grasshoppers. Termites and grubs are also popular. As the need for food rises, we should all try eating bugs. There are good reasons to do so.

4   Insects are good for you. Many kinds of bugs, such as mealworms, provide as much protein as fish or meat. They have vitamins and minerals. They provide as much calcium and iron as milk or green vegetables, such as kale.

5   Raising sheep or cattle for meat takes a lot of land, water, and feed. Around the world, about a third of the land goes to farming and livestock. Raising cows and other animals is costly and wasteful. It takes hundreds of gallons of water to produce one pound of meat. Farmers can raise insects almost anywhere at a much lower cost and with fewer resources. Insects can feed on weeds, food waste, table scraps, almost anything. They can also be harvested in the wild. When a cloud of locusts lands in a field, for example, it is free food.

(continued)

6   Treating insects as food can also help fight climate change. They do not harm the environment. So why not try a deep-fried cricket today? Or a chocolate-covered ant? Or some fried bees? You might just grow to like them, and you'll be helping our Earth.

1. **What is the author's main argument in this passage?**

   (A) The world's population is growing.

   (B) We should eat more insects as food.

   (C) Earth is getting warmer every year.

   (D) We should stop raising large animals for food.

2. **According to the author, what kinds of bugs are most popular as food? Name <u>two</u> kinds.**

   _____

   _____

3. **What evidence does the author give to show that many people eat bugs? Write the sentence from the passage.**

   _____

   _____

4. **In which sentences from the passage does the author give reasons to support the main argument? Choose <u>three</u> answers.**

   (A) "Some people say that grasshoppers have a nutty taste."

   (B) "Not long ago, the United Nations (UN) issued a report on world hunger."

   (C) "Insects are good for you."

   (D) "Farmers can raise insects almost anywhere at a much lower cost and with fewer resources."

   (E) "When a cloud of locusts lands in a field, for example, it is free food."

   (F) "Treating insects as food can also help fight climate change."

Name: _____   Date: _____

What Time Is Noon?

1   At any given moment, it's nighttime in half of the world. In the other half, it's day. As Earth turns, time varies in different parts of the world. For many centuries, differences in time did not matter. People did not travel far enough or fast enough to be affected by time differences. They only cared what time it was in their own city or town.

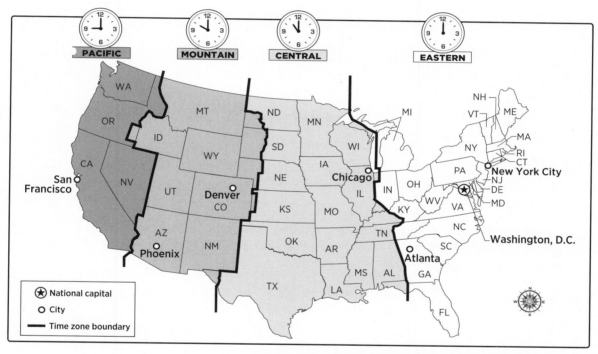

The continental United States is divided into four time zones.

2   But that changed when railroads began carrying people long distances. How do you make a train schedule when the places you go have different times? The railroads needed a way to coordinate times in different places. In 1883, U.S. railroads solved the problem by creating four "time zones." The system became official in 1918, and the rest of the world adopted time zones soon after that.

3   Today, the continental United States still has four time zones, as shown on the map. (Alaska and Hawaii are located in different zones.) Within each zone, the time is the same for everyone. This means that when it's noon in New York City, it's also noon in Atlanta. They are both in the Eastern Time Zone. However, when it is noon in New York, it's only 9:00 A.M. in San Francisco. That city is in the Pacific Time Zone, three zones away.

(continued)

4   The world has 24 time zones. As you travel west, you subtract one hour for each time zone. Going east, you add one hour. When it is noon in New York, it is midnight in parts of Asia. Russia, the world's largest country, has 11 time zones. China has only one time zone, even though it is the fourth largest country by area. The Chinese decided that having one time zone would make everyone in the country feel connected.

5   Dividing the world into time zones made travel and communication much easier for everyone. Now, trains and planes and everything else can run on schedule.

---

1. **The author of this passage claims that time differences did not matter for many centuries. Which sentence from the first paragraph best supports this claim?**

    (A) "At any given moment, it's nighttime in half of the world."

    (B) "As Earth turns, time varies in different parts of the world."

    (C) "People did not travel far enough or fast enough to be affected by time differences."

    (D) "They only cared what time it was in their own city or town."

2. **Which sentence in paragraph 2 explains why U.S. railroads created time zones? Underline the sentence.**

    But that changed when railroads began carrying people long distances. How do you make a train schedule when the places you go have different times? The railroads needed a way to coordinate times in different places. In 1883, U.S. railroads solved the problem by creating four "time zones." The system became official in 1918, and the rest of the world adopted time zones soon after that.

3. **According to the map, when it is 5:00 P.M. in Atlanta, what time is it in Phoenix?**

    _____

4. **Which sentence in paragraph 4 explains why China has only one time zone? Write the sentence.**

    _____

    _____

Informational Texts for Striving Readers: Grade 5 © 2021 by Michael Priestley, Scholastic Inc. • page 58

Name: _____   Date: _____

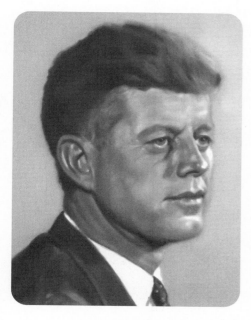

John F. Kennedy was the 35th president of the United States.

Adapted from
"The Moon Speech,"
by President John F. Kennedy

Just one year after the first manned space launch, President Kennedy gave this speech about the space program. He spoke in Houston, Texas, on September 12, 1962.

1   Those who came before us made certain that this country rode the first waves of the industrial revolutions and modern invention. This generation does not intend to founder in the backwash of the coming age of space. We mean to be a part of it. We mean to lead it. For the eyes of the world now look into space, to the moon and to the planets beyond. And we have vowed that we shall see it governed by a banner of freedom and peace.

2   Yet the vows of this Nation can only be fulfilled if we in this Nation are first. And, therefore, we intend to be first.

3   We set sail on this new sea because there is new knowledge to be gained, and new rights to be won. And they must be won and used for the progress of all people. For space science has no conscience of its own. Whether it will become a force for good or ill depends on man.

4   But why, some say, the moon? Why choose this as our goal? And they may well ask why climb the highest mountain? Why, 35 years ago, fly the Atlantic?

5   We choose to go to the moon. We choose to go to the moon in this decade and do the other things, not because they are easy, but because they are hard. That goal will serve to organize the best of our energies and skills. That challenge is one that we are willing to accept, and one we intend to win.

(continued)

6   Within these last 19 months at least 45 satellites have circled the earth. Some 40 of them were "made in the United States of America." Transit satellites are helping our ships at sea to steer a safer course. *Tiros* satellites give us warnings of hurricanes and storms. They will do the same for forest fires and icebergs. We have had our failures, but so have others.

7   To be sure, we are behind, and will be behind for some time in manned flight. But we do not intend to stay behind. And in this decade, we shall make up and move ahead.

8   The growth of our science and education will be enriched by new knowledge of our universe and environment. The space effort itself has already created a great number of new companies and tens of thousands of new jobs.

9   To be sure, all this costs us all a good deal of money. This year's space budget is three times what it was in January 1961. It is greater than the space budget of the previous eight years combined.

10   However, I think we're going to do it. And I think that we must pay what needs to be paid. I don't think we ought to waste any money, but I think we ought to do the job. And it will be done before the end of this decade.

11   Many years ago the great British explorer George Mallory was asked why did he want to climb Mount Everest. He said, "Because it is there."

12   Well, space is there, and we're going to climb it.

---

1. What is President Kennedy's main argument in this speech?

(A) Americans have made the best satellites.

(B) The U.S. should be the first to go to the moon.

(C) Sending people into space costs a lot of money.

(D) No other country will be allowed to control the moon.

2. Which sentence in the first paragraph states America's goal for the moon? Underline the sentence.

Those who came before us made certain that this country rode the first waves of the industrial revolutions and modern invention. This generation does not intend to founder in the backwash of the coming age of space. We mean to be a part of it. We mean to lead it. For the eyes of the world now look into space, to the moon and to the planets beyond. And we have vowed that we shall see it governed by a banner of freedom and peace.

(continued)

Informational Texts for Striving Readers: Grade 5 © 2021 by Michael Priestley, Scholastic Inc. • page 60

Adapted from "The Moon Speech"

3. **According to President Kennedy, how did satellites benefit the U.S.? Choose <u>two</u> answers.**

   (A) They helped ships steer a safer course.

   (B) They served as weapons against enemies.

   (C) They prevented forest fires from spreading.

   (D) They gave warnings about hurricanes and storms.

   (E) They helped scientists measure distances accurately.

4. **This question has two parts. Answer Part A. Then answer Part B.**

   PART A

   What claim does President Kennedy make about the space program?

   (A) It will not be too expensive.

   (B) It will make the country rich.

   (C) It will succeed in two or three years.

   (D) It will help the country in many ways.

   PART B

   Which <u>two</u> sentences from the passage support the answer in Part A?

   (A) "We choose to go to the moon in this decade and do the other things, not because they are easy, but because they are hard."

   (B) "And in this decade, we shall make up and move ahead."

   (C) "The growth of our science and education will be enriched by new knowledge of our universe and environment."

   (D) "The space effort itself has already created a great number of new companies and tens of thousands of new jobs."

   (E) "This year's space budget is three times what it was in January 1961."

Name: _____ Date: _____

Hot! Hot! Hot!

1   If you've ever eaten chili peppers, then you know why we call them "hot!"
A spicy chili pepper can make your mouth feel like it's on fire. You might
even start sweating or crying. Even so, many
people love chili peppers and eat them
every day. They are important to
many food cultures.

2   There are more than
50,000 types of peppers.
And new types are being
developed all the time.
Peppers come in all colors
and shapes, from spicy
jalapeño to mild yellow bell
peppers. Some have a smoky flavor,
and some are sweet. Others will make
your eyes water. Chili peppers are the hot ones.
People use them to make
sauces and add spice
to food.

Chili peppers come in
different degrees of "hotness."

3   Chili peppers come
from Mexico and
Central America. Spanish
explorers first brought
them back to Europe
from the Caribbean.
From there, they spread
across the globe. Today,
they're very popular in
many places.

(continued)
(continued)

The Carolina Reaper

Every few years, someone creates a
new type of pepper that's spicier
than ever. But the Carolina
Reaper has been at the top of
the list since 2013, when it was named the hottest
pepper in the world. To give you an idea, the Reaper
is more than 200 times hotter than a jalapeño.
(That's the kind of tongue-burning pepper used in
many Mexican foods.) The degree of hotness in
peppers depends on the amount of *capsaicin* they
have. That is what makes a pepper hot, and the
Reaper has plenty of it. A man named Ed Currie
developed this new pepper in the southern United
States. It's less than two inches long and has a pointy
tail. But be careful if you decide to give it a try.
Touching this chili pepper with bare hands can burn
your skin, and eating it raw is not recommended!

4   Eating chili peppers offers many benefits, if you can handle the heat. They pack plenty of Vitamin C and Vitamin A, which help keep you from getting sick. They can help reduce inflammation in the body. They also provide Vitamin E. A diet with a lot of chili peppers can lower the risk of heart disease. And, of course, they can also help clear a stuffy nose!

1. **According to the sidebar, one kind of chili pepper can —**
    A make you cry
    B burn your skin
    C make you sweat
    D clear a stuffy nose

2. **Which sentence in paragraph 2 is supported by information in the sidebar? Underline the sentence.**

    There are more than 50,000 types of peppers. And new types are being developed all the time. Peppers come in all colors and shapes, from spicy jalapeño to mild yellow bell peppers. Some have a smoky flavor, and some are sweet. Others will make your eyes water. Chili peppers are the hot ones. People use them to make sauces and add spice to food.

3. **How is the Carolina Reaper different from other peppers? Write your answer.**

    _____

    _____

4. **What piece of information does the sidebar add to the passage?**
    A The ingredient that makes peppers spicy is *capsaicin*.
    B Chili peppers are high in Vitamins A, C, and E.
    C There are more than 50,000 types of peppers.
    D Chili peppers can be used in cooking.

Name: _____ Date: _____

Slovenia: A Land of Fairy Tales

Predjama Castle in Slovenia

1   Imagine a place with green forests and bright blue rivers. It has lakes so clean that you can see all the way to the bottom. It has beaches by the sea and ski trails in the mountains. Stone castles rise up out of the valleys. Even the cities seem to dwell in magical forests. It sounds like a fairy tale, but this place is real. It is called Slovenia.

2   Slovenia is a small country in Europe. It was part of Yugoslavia until 1991, when it gained independence. It shares borders with Austria, Hungary, Italy, and Croatia. By area, it is a bit smaller than the state of New Jersey.

3   For such a small country, Slovenia has some fascinating geography. Part of the country touches the Adriatic Sea and its sunny beaches. Another part edges up to the Alps, the highest mountains in Europe. They offer places to ski, sled, and snowshoe. But the distance between the sea and the mountains is small. One could ski in the mountains and swim in the sea on the same day.

4   Besides the sea and the Alps, the middle of Slovenia features gorgeous valleys, rivers, and lakes. The Soca River is one of the most beautiful rivers in Europe. Its blue-green water is a very unusual color, like emeralds.

(continued)

Slovenia's Baby Dragons

Deep in Slovenia's Postojna Cave lives the *olm*. This special animal is a kind of salamander. It is sometimes called "the human fish" or "baby dragon." The olm has very light pink skin, a flat head, and four small legs. Because it has adapted to the dark, its skin is so thin that it seems to glow. It's also blind. The olm can live up to a hundred years, and it can grow up to a foot long. It eats worms, tiny shrimp, and snails, but amazingly, the olm can survive up to ten years without food! Hundreds of thousands of tourists travel to the Postojna Cave each year. Many go to see the deep caverns, the colored rocks, and the rock bridges. But some go just to see the "baby dragons."

Informational Texts for Striving Readers: Grade 5 © 2021 by Michael Priestley, Scholastic Inc. • page 64

People travel to the Soca Valley for many activities. They go whitewater rafting, kayaking, fishing, and zip-lining. Because of its beauty, parts of a fairy-tale movie based on *The Chronicles of Narnia* were filmed there in 2007.

5   Slovenia is also famous for what lies below the surface. The country has more than 8,000 caves. Many of them are popular places to visit. In one area, a river called the Reka disappears into a cave. It flows 24 miles underground and then comes back up. Another famous cave system, the Krizna Jama, has 22 connected underground lakes.

6   Beyond the natural attractions of Slovenia, its cities are special, too. They are very safe, friendly, and green. Its capital city is Ljubljana. It has roads made of white stones, a river running through the middle, and even a castle. About 75 percent of the city has trees and green spaces. In 2016, it was officially named the European Green Capital. It is truly a fairy-tale setting.

1. **Which sentence in the first paragraph best supports the idea that Slovenia is a "land of fairy tales"? Write the sentence.**

_____

_____

2. **What natural wonders can be found only in Slovenia? Choose <u>two</u> answers.**

   (A) Soca River   (D) Postojna Cave
   (B) Adriatic Sea   (E) underground lakes
   (C) the Alps

3. **What tourist attraction in Slovenia is described in the sidebar but <u>not</u> in the main passage?**

   (A) Krizna Jama   (C) Postojna Cave
   (B) Reka River   (D) Ljubljana castle

4. **What piece of information about Slovenia does the sidebar add to the passage?**

   (A) It has more than 8,000 caves.   (C) It borders the Alps and the Adriatic.
   (B) It is home to a unique animal.   (D) Its capital city has large green spaces.

5. **What is unusual about the "baby dragons" of Slovenia? Describe <u>two</u> things.**

_____

_____

Name: _____ Date: _____

Very Strange Marathons

1   Every four years, thousands of athletes from around the world take part in the Summer Olympics. These athletes compete in cycling, diving, canoeing, archery, and many other events that test their abilities. One of the top endurance events is the *marathon*, in which the best distance runners run 26.2 miles. But the marathon wasn't always an important part of the Olympics. In fact, the first few attempts ended in disaster.

Runners in the 1904 Olympics

2   The first modern Olympics took place in Athens, Greece, in 1896. At the time, long-distance running was not common. Only 17 men competed in the marathon. Most of them had never run such a long distance before. Only nine runners finished the race. The man who finished in third place got disqualified when officials found out he had ridden in a carriage part of the way.

3   The next summer Olympics took place in 1904 in St. Louis, Missouri. A total of 32 runners started the race. With temperatures over 90 degrees, the runners had a hard time racing in the dust and heat. They did not have enough access to water. More than half of the racers quit before finishing.

4   The runners who managed the heat had other problems. Wild dogs chased one runner from South Africa a mile off course. Another runner, Felix Carbajal from Cuba, got hungry along the way. He stopped and ate some green apples. He got terrible stomach cramps and had to stop to take a nap.

(continued)

Tips for Safely Running a Marathon

Physical Training. Experts recommend training at least a year before running a marathon. Training should include short- and long-distance runs, strength workouts, and stretching.

Mental Training. Mental training can help runners get through pain and boredom without giving up.

Hydration. Runners need to drink a lot of water to avoid dehydration. They need even more water in hot weather. Special running vests and belts help runners carry water with them. Most long races today also have water stations.

Fuel. A good diet helps runners keep their energy up. During the race, runners should eat snacks or sports gels that are easy to digest.

Rest. Runners should rest between training days. This helps the body recover. Getting enough sleep is also important.

Informational Texts for Striving Readers: Grade 5 © 2021 by Michael Priestley, Scholastic Inc. • page 66

5   American runner Fred Lorz crossed the finish line faster than anyone expected. The crowd cheered for him until they found out he had ridden more than ten miles in a car. He was disqualified. Another American, Thomas Hicks, stopped to eat a mixture of chemicals and egg whites. He believed that it would help him run faster. But the mixture was actually dangerous and could have killed him. His skin turned gray and he began to see things that weren't there. He kept running anyway, but he almost passed out before the finish. His trainers helped carry him over the finish line while he moved his feet back and forth in the air. Officials named him the winner.

6   After this strange marathon in 1904, many people thought the event should be removed from the Olympics. They said that running such a long distance was too hard. But in 1908, the marathon was held again at the London Olympics. It was another disaster. Many runners quit the race. Some ran in the wrong direction. Others got thrown out for cheating.

7   Since then, long-distance running has become more popular. In 2018, 1.1 million people ran in marathons around the world. Today, they are well-organized events. But those first few Olympic marathons will not be forgotten.

1. **What did the Olympic marathons in 1896 and 1904 have in common? Choose <u>two</u> answers.**
    - (A) Heat and dust made running difficult.
    - (B) One of the top finishers got disqualified.
    - (C) About half of the runners failed to finish.
    - (D) Fewer than 20 runners entered the race.
    - (E) The course went through dangerous areas.

2. **Based on information in the sidebar, what is one reason so few runners finished the 1896 marathon in Athens?**
    - (A) The runners did not get enough sleep.
    - (B) The runners did not have the right shoes.
    - (C) The runners could not breathe due to dust.
    - (D) The runners had not trained for long distances.

3. **Based on the tips in the sidebar, what did many of the runners probably suffer from during the 1904 marathon in St. Louis?**
    - (A) dehydration
    - (B) blisters
    - (C) sore knees
    - (D) frostbite

4. **Which tip from the sidebar would have helped Felix Carbajal during the 1904 Olympic marathon? Write your answer.**

    _____

Name: _____   Date: _____

2,000 Years of Fireworks

1   Every year for the Fourth of July, many Americans celebrate independence by shooting off fireworks. This custom began in Philadelphia in 1777 during the American Revolution. That year, ships fired 13 cannons to honor the 13 colonies.

2   Fireworks were most likely invented in China more than 2,000 years ago. People tossed sticks of bamboo onto a fire. Bamboo grows with a tube-like stem that is mostly hollow. When heated, air pockets in the bamboo make loud popping noises. Some believed that the loud noises would keep away evil spirits.

3   Hundreds of years later, people began to fill the bamboo with chemicals, like gun powder. That caused an even louder blast. Paper tubes eventually replaced the bamboo. Later, chemists figured out how to fire them into the air and make the fireworks go where they wanted.

4   In England long ago, the people who set up fireworks entertained the crowds. They told jokes and had fun. These "green men" wore caps made from leaves. The leaves protected their heads from sparks. In the 1830s, Italians became the first to add special salts to the tubes. These salts added colors to the fireworks we enjoy today.

1. **In what country were the first fireworks set off?**

   _____

2. **Which sentence in paragraph 2 tells why bamboo was used to make fireworks? Write the sentence.**

   _____

   _____

3. **In England, why did the "green men" wear caps made from leaves?**
   - (A) The caps made the people laugh.
   - (B) The leaves had special salts in them.
   - (C) The caps kept sparks off their heads.
   - (D) The leaves added color to the fireworks.

Informational Texts for Striving Readers: Grade 5 © 2021 by Michael Priestley, Scholastic Inc. • page 68

Name: _____ Date: _____

A Wild West Town

The Bodie "ghost town" became a National Historic Landmark in 1961.

1   The California Gold Rush began in 1849. Within a few years, 300,000 people traveled to California from around the world. Mining towns popped up all over the place. But in less than ten years, all of the gold that miners could dig by hand was gone. By 1858, most of the miners had left, too. Towns that boomed during the Gold Rush became ghost towns.

2   One man named W. S. Bodey did not quit. With three friends, he headed off to find his fortune. One day in 1859, the men stopped on a desert bluff near the Nevada border. Scratching around in the dirt, Bodey uncovered what he had spent a decade hunting for. He struck gold. Sadly, his luck didn't last. A few months later, he got caught in a snowstorm and froze. In his honor, his friends named the area "Bodey Bluff."

3   People came and went from the bluff but did not get rich. Then, in 1874, the walls of a large mining pit caved in. Where the earth tore away, the miners found a large vein of pure gold. Word of the discovery spread quickly. More than 8,000 people raced to the tiny town. Some dug for gold. Others built houses, hotels, banks, schools, and stores. The town had a union hall for meetings, shows, dances, and funerals. Two churches in town served as schools for the children.

4   The town, now called "Bodie," became a wild town filled with lawbreakers. It was a dangerous place to go, even for tough miners. By 1915, however, most of the gold seemed to be gone. The miners moved out, leaving behind another empty ghost town.

(continued)

5   Most of the other Gold Rush towns had burned down, blown over, or simply fallen apart. Perhaps that is why people decided it was important to save Bodie. They wanted a place where visitors could see what life was like in the old mining towns. So they preserved Bodie just as it was.

6   Today, we can walk along Bodie's deserted streets. We can peek through store windows and see supplies on the shelves. We can look into classrooms at old desks and chairs and books. In some of the homes, the tables are still set for supper. Everything is covered in a thick layer of dust.

7   Some people believe that more than $150 million worth of gold is still buried in Bodie. The town may be worth even more as a piece of history.

---

1. **Why was the town named after W. S. Bodey?**

   (A) He lived there.   (C) He built the town.
   (B) He found gold there.   (D) He got caught in a storm.

2. **Which sentence in paragraph 3 tells why people hurried to Bodie after the walls of a pit caved in? Write the sentence.**

   _____

   _____

3. **Bodie became known as a wild town because —**

   (A) it had a large mining pit   (C) it had shows, dances, and funerals
   (B) about 8,000 people moved there   (D) many people did not obey the laws

4. **Which sentences in the passage tell why some people wanted to save Bodie? Choose two answers.**

   (A) "Most of the other Gold Rush towns had burned down, blown over, or simply fallen apart."
   (B) "They wanted a place where visitors could see what life was like in the old mining towns."
   (C) "Today, we can walk along Bodie's deserted streets."
   (D) "Everything is covered in a thick layer of dust."
   (E) "Some people believe that more than $150 million worth of gold is still buried in Bodie."

Name: _____ Date: _____

Animal Invaders

1   In 1883, farmers in Hawaii had a problem. Rats were eating their sugar cane and destroying the crop. The farmers needed help. They heard that mongooses fed on rats. So they brought some of the weasel-like animals to Hawaii to save their sugar cane. But the farmers did not know that mongooses hunted during the day, while the rats came out only at night. So the mongooses left the rats alone. Instead, they ate all the birds and turtle eggs.

2   The mongoose is an example of an *invasive animal*. It's called "invasive" because it lives in a place it doesn't belong. In its new home, it has no natural enemies and cannot be controlled. And it causes a lot of damage.

3   Invasive animals are everywhere. Another group of sugar-cane farmers took 102 cane toads from Puerto Rico to Australia. They expected the toads to prey on cane beetles that were eating the sugar cane. Instead, the giant toads wandered off and multiplied. The country now has more than 1.5 billion of these toads, which are poisonous to any animals that eat them.

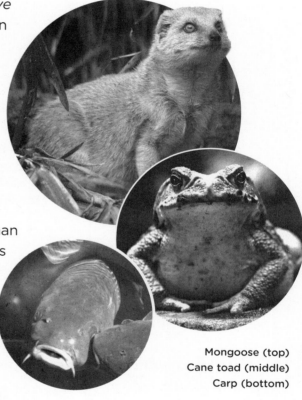

Mongoose (top)
Cane toad (middle)
Carp (bottom)

4   Australia has had more than its share of invasive animals. In 1840, British settlers brought in some camels from India. They used these pack animals for transportation. Then, when cars and trucks came along, people set the camels loose. Now, more than one million wild camels wander through farmlands. They eat the plants and destroy property.

5   Much the same thing happened with rabbits. Australia had no rabbits until 1857. British settlers brought some to the continent for hunting and food. But rabbits multiply rapidly, and they had no real enemies in Australia. Now there are millions of these mammals. They eat crops and destroy young trees, causing problems.

(continued)

6   The United States has plenty of these problems, too. For example, in the 1970s, fish farmers brought in four kinds of carp from Asia. These large fish were supposed to eat weeds and algae in the fish ponds and canals. But the carp escaped and got into the Mississippi River. Now they have spread up and down the river. They drive out almost all the native fish. Experts worry that these carp will get into the Great Lakes and ruin the fishing industry.

7   Worldwide, the list of invasive animals is long and growing. We cannot control all future invasions. But we should learn our lessons from what has happened in the past and not bring animals where they don't belong.

1. **According to the passage, which of these are invasive animals in Australia? Choose two answers.**

    (A) rat   (D) rabbit
    (B) camel   (E) cane beetle
    (C) turtle

2. **Which sentence from the first paragraph explains why mongooses did not help the sugar-cane farmers in Hawaii? Write the sentence.**

    _____

    _____

3. **In the U.S., what "invader" is causing problems in the Mississippi River?**

    _____

4. **Which sentence from the passage tells one reason invasive animals cause so much damage in their new homes?**

    (A) "It's called 'invasive' because it lives in a place it doesn't belong."

    (B) "In its new home, it has no natural enemies and cannot be controlled."

    (C) "Worldwide, the list of invasive animals is long and growing."

    (D) "But we should learn our lessons from what has happened in the past and not bring animals where they don't belong."

Name: _____   Date: _____

Read each passage and answer the questions that follow.

PASSAGE A

A Juggling Act

1   One of the most popular acts in the circus is juggling. Men and women in costumes keep several objects in the air by tossing and catching them. They move quickly, always in motion. They may toss balls, rings, or clubs. Some experts might juggle knives or torches on fire. The best performers might juggle while riding a unicycle or walking on a tightrope. They put on an amazing show.

A juggler can keep three or more objects in the air.

2   Juggling is one of the oldest forms of entertainment. Ancient drawings on tombs show that juggling was part of Egyptian culture around 4,000 years ago. In China, around 600 BCE, warriors practiced juggling before they went to battle. One of the most famous warriors of that time was Xiong Yiliao. One story says he juggled nine balls in front of the enemy before a fight. His amazing skill scared them away. Romans during the time of the Roman Empire (31 BCE–476 CE) also liked juggling. Nobles often hired jugglers to entertain at their courts and parties.

3   Today, many people practice juggling as a **pastime**. They might juggle at home or with friends. Some enter juggling contests. It's a fun hobby but also offers other benefits. Since it requires a lot of focus, it's a great tool for relaxation. It helps improve eye-hand coordination. It's also a good exercise for arms and shoulders. Over a few months, juggling can help boost brain power and concentration.

4   Next time you feel bored, grab any three objects you can find and give juggling a try!

A Juggling Act

1. **What is the main purpose of this passage?**

    (A) to explain how to juggle

    (B) to tell a story about a circus

    (C) to convince people to try juggling

    (D) to give information about juggling

2. **Which detail from the passage supports the idea that juggling was once used for war?**

    (A) "Ancient drawings on tombs show that juggling was part of Egyptian culture around 4,000 years ago."

    (B) "One story says he juggled nine balls in front of the enemy before a fight. His amazing skill scared them away."

    (C) "Romans during the time of the Roman Empire (31 BCE–476 CE) also liked juggling."

    (D) "Nobles often hired jugglers to entertain at their courts and parties."

3. **What is the meaning of the word *pastime* in paragraph 3?**

    (A) part of a circus

    (B) a job that pays well

    (C) something fun to do

    (D) a way to honor someone

4. **According to the passage, what are some benefits of juggling as a hobby? Choose <u>two</u> answers.**

    (A) It is good exercise.

    (B) It can scare people.

    (C) It helps people relax.

    (D) It improves eyesight.

    (E) It makes people laugh.

PASSAGE B
Meet the Pronghorn

1   You may have heard the song "Home on the Range" about the American West—"where the deer and the antelope play." That "antelope" is actually a pronghorn. This animal is native to the prairies of North America. It has reddish-brown fur with white markings. It **resembles** a deer in size and shape. But the pronghorn has some characteristics that make it unique.

A pronghorn's horns can grow up to 10 inches long.

2   The pronghorn is the only remaining member of a family of mammals that lived long ago. Most of them died out after the last Ice Age, along with saber-toothed cats, mammoths, and giant sloths. Not only has the pronghorn survived, but it still looks much the same.

3   One special characteristic of the pronghorn is its speed. It is the second-fastest land animal on Earth. It can run as fast as 60 miles per hour. Only the cheetah runs faster. But the pronghorn can keep running at high speed longer. Its hooves have two long "toes" that help it absorb shock. It runs with its mouth open to take in more oxygen.

4   Another unique part of the pronghorn is its horns. They are actually a cross between horns and antlers, which differ in some ways. Antlers are made of bone and fall off before winter. The animals shed their antlers and then grow new ones. Antlers have two or more points, while horns have only one. And horns do not fall off. Instead, they keep growing and then wear down. The pronghorn is the only animal that has horns with more than one point that also fall off once a year.

5   Pronghorns eat only plants, such as grass, sagebrush, shrubs, and sometimes even cacti. They absorb water from the plants they eat. They can live for days, or even weeks, without drinking water.

6   Pronghorns always stay alert for danger. They have large eyes that help them spot danger up to four miles away. When they spot danger, they raise the white fur near the tail to signal one another. But pronghorns are also curious. If they see something moving in the distance, such as a flag waving, they will often trot over to investigate.

7   In the fall and winter, pronghorns travel in large herds. It's an awesome sight to see as many as a thousand of them migrating together across the American West, where the deer and the pronghorns play.

Meet the Pronghorn

5.   This question has two parts. Answer Part A. Then answer Part B.

   PART A What is the central idea of this passage?

   (A) Many species of animals did not survive the last Ice Age.

   (B) Pronghorns are animals with some unique characteristics.

   (C) The cheetah is the only land animal faster than a pronghorn.

   (D) Pronghorns get their name from the forked horns on their head.

   PART B Which detail best supports the central idea in Part A?

   (A) "This animal is native to the prairies of North America."

   (B) "It runs with its mouth open to take in more oxygen."

   (C) "The pronghorn is the only animal that has horns with more than one point that also fall off once a year."

   (D) "Pronghorns eat only plants, such as grass, sagebrush, shrubs, and sometimes even cacti."

6.   **What is the meaning of the word *resembles* in the first paragraph?**

   (A) looks like   (C) is related to

   (B) differs from   (D) runs faster than

7.   **What are <u>two</u> differences between horns and antlers?**

   (A) Horns point to the back; antlers point to the front.

   (B) Horns are one color; antlers are more than one color.

   (C) Horns continually grow and wear down; antlers fall off.

   (D) Horns have one point; antlers have two or more points.

   (E) Horns are dull and rounded; antlers are sharp and pointed.

8.   **Which sentence from the passage gives the author's view of pronghorns?**

   (A) "Pronghorns always stay alert for danger."

   (B) "If they see something moving in the distance, such as a flag waving, they will often trot over to investigate."

   (C) "In the fall and winter, pronghorns travel in large herds."

   (D) "It's an awesome sight to see as many as a thousand of them migrating together across the American West, where the deer and the pronghorns play."

PASSAGE C

Strange Creatures of the Deep

1   Some of the strangest creatures on our planet live in the deepest parts of the ocean. Their bodies have special adaptations to help them survive in these very dark and cold places.

2   One such adaptation is *bioluminescence*. Because the sun cannot reach the deep ocean, it is always dark. But some creatures that live there can make their own light. These animals release a chemical that reacts with oxygen to create a glow.

3   One animal that uses bioluminescence is the deep-sea anglerfish. It has a long, thin piece sticking out of its head. At the tip is a bright light. The light attracts fish, shrimp, and other small sea creatures. When they move close, the anglerfish gobbles them up.

4   Many jellyfish also have bioluminescence. They often use their glowing bodies to defend themselves. Some jellyfish can turn a bright flash on and off to confuse or scare predators. The lanternfish also creates its own glow. It has a light in the front of its face that acts like a headlight.

The anglerfish (top) uses a lure to catch other fish.

The gulper eel (bottom) has a huge mouth that opens wide.

5   Another deep-sea adaptation is an extra-large mouth. A number of creatures, such as the dragon fish and gulper eel, have huge mouths. At these depths, prey is **sparse**. Because food is so hard to find, fish need to be able to eat as much as possible in one bite. In addition, fish such as the anglerfish and viperfish also have very long teeth. These teeth prevent the prey from escaping.

(continued)

6.   Some other strange creatures have adapted to live on the ocean floor itself. The giant isopod, for example, is related to the rounded gray pill bugs you might see in a garden. It has seven pairs of legs to help it move and can grow to more than 16 inches long. Another is the "spaghetti monster," a weird-looking relative of jellyfish. It lives at a depth of about 4,000 feet. It has numerous tentacles that look like noodles. These tentacles catch tiny prey as the beast moves along the ocean floor.

7.   Most of the ocean deep has not yet been explored. Only a handful of humans have ever seen it. However, new developments in technology have allowed scientists to take pictures at great depths. That is how we have found some of these creatures. Scientists believe there may be many others yet to be discovered.

More than 60 percent of Earth's surface is covered by water at least a mile deep. The deepest part of the ocean is called the Challenger Deep, in the Pacific Ocean. It is almost seven miles deep. Sunlight cannot reach below a thousand meters, or about six-tenths of a mile, so it is always dark. The temperature of the water on the ocean floor stays just above freezing (32°F).

9.   **This question has two parts. Answer Part A. Then answer Part B.**

PART A

What is the central idea of this passage?

(A) Very few animals can live in the deep ocean.

(B) Some creatures have adapted to live deep in the sea.

(C) The deepest parts of the sea are dark and mysterious.

(D) Many animals that live in the deep ocean make their own light.

Informational Texts for Striving Readers: Grade 5 © 2021 by Michael Priestley, Scholastic Inc. • page 78

PRACTICE TEST

Strange Creatures of the Deep

PART B

Which sentence from the passage best supports the answer in Part A?

A "Some of the strangest creatures on our planet live in the deepest parts of the ocean."

B "Because the sun cannot reach the deep ocean, it is always very dark."

C "A number of creatures, such as the dragon fish and gulper eel, have huge mouths."

D "Most of the ocean deep has not yet been explored."

10. **Which evidence from the passage supports the idea that some deep-sea creatures use bioluminescence to catch food?**

A "But some creatures that live there can make their own light."

B "These animals release a chemical that reacts with oxygen to create a glow."

C "One animal that uses bioluminescence is the deep-sea anglerfish."

D "The light attracts fish, shrimp, and other small sea creatures."

11. **Which sentence in paragraph 4 tells how jellyfish use bioluminescence? Underline the sentence.**

    Many jellyfish also have bioluminescence. They often use their glowing bodies to defend themselves. Some jellyfish can turn a bright flash on and off to confuse or scare predators. The lanternfish also creates its own glow. It has a light in the front of its face that acts like a headlight.

12. **Which phrase in paragraph 5 gives a clue to the meaning of *sparse*?**

A "extra-large mouth"

B "hard to find"

C "in one bite"

D "very long teeth"

13. **What point does the author make in <u>both</u> the passage and the sidebar?**

A The deep ocean receives no sunlight.

B Much of the planet is covered by deep water.

C The deep ocean has very little food for predators.

D Many kinds of fish in the deep ocean have huge mouths.

Informational Texts for Striving Readers: Grade 5 © 2021 by Michael Priestley, Scholastic Inc. • page 79

PASSAGE D
Exploring the Ocean Floor

1   The bottom of the ocean has long been a mystery to humans. So far, we have explored only about 20 percent of the world's ocean floor. Now, new technology **enables** explorers to go deeper than ever. On each dive, they find creatures that have never been seen. They also find some surprising objects.

The Five Deeps Expedition

2   On August 24, 2019, Victor Vescovo reached the bottom of the Molloy Trench. That is the deepest part of the Arctic Ocean. With that trip, Vescovo had reached the deepest point in each of the five oceans. One goal was to map new parts of the sea floor. Along the way, Vescovo and his crew saw some unusual things. They found some new kinds of prawns, which are like shrimp. In the Pacific Ocean, they dove to the Challenger Deep, the deepest place on Earth. That is nearly seven miles down. There, Vescovo found plastic bags and candy wrappers. Humans had never been to that part of the ocean before, but they had left their mark.

Other Discoveries

3   Over the years, people have found other strange things in the sea. They include gas masks, trucks, cannonballs, and pirate ships. In the Mediterranean Sea, divers found a chest full of medicine from ancient Rome. Off the coast of Florida, explorers found rocket engines from the *Apollo 11* program. The engines fell back to Earth after their launch in 1969 and sank in the ocean to a depth of 16,000 feet.

4   In 1985, divers found a train graveyard in the Atlantic Ocean. Two steam engines from the 1850s sit on the bottom of the sea. They are covered with rust. Oddly, there is no record of these trains ever being built or lost. Scientists think the trains might have fallen off a ship on their way to Europe.

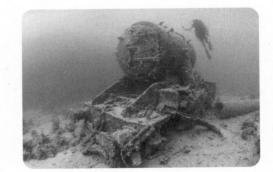

Explorers found an underwater train graveyard off the coast of New Jersey.

5   In 2020, a team of scientists made a truly surprising find. Off the coast of Greenland, they discovered a coral garden. The garden sits about 1,600 feet underwater. It is home to at least 44,000 organisms. Coral most often grows near the surface in warm waters, partly because it needs sunlight. But Greenland is near the North Pole. The water is always cold and dark. Scientists plan to study this coral garden for years to come.

Exploring the Ocean Floor

14. In the first paragraph, what does the word *enables* mean?

(A) urges

(B) allows

(C) teaches

(D) prevents

15. What text structure does the author use in the section titled "Other Discoveries"?

(A) comparison and contrast

(B) problem and solution

(C) chronological order

(D) cause and effect

16. Where was the train graveyard found?

(A) near Greenland

(B) in the Arctic Ocean

(C) near New Jersey

(D) off the Florida coast

The next three questions are about both Passage C and Passage D.

17. Which of these ideas are found in <u>both</u> Passage C and Passage D? Choose <u>two</u> answers.

(A) Explorers have discovered some strange things in the ocean.

(B) Victor Vescovo was surprised to find plastic bags and trash on the ocean floor.

(C) Some deep-sea creatures have a special adaptation called *bioluminescence*.

(D) Coral gardens usually grow near the surface, mainly because coral needs sunlight.

(E) The deepest place in any ocean is Challenger Deep, nearly seven miles down.

18. In what way are these two passages <u>different</u>?

(A) Passage C says that new technology helps ocean explorers, but Passage D does not mention technology.

(B) Passage C describes the Five Deeps Expedition, but Passage D does not.

(C) Passage C gives information about Challenger Deep, but Passage D does not.

(D) Passage C describes only animals found in the deep ocean, but Passage D mainly describes objects.

19. Which of these statements would the authors of <u>both</u> passages most likely agree with?

(A) Exploring the ocean has little value to scientists.

(B) People have left trash in every part of the ocean.

(C) The strangest things in the sea are human-made.

(D) Most of the ocean floor has not yet been explored.

PASSAGE E

Guiding Stars

1   Thousands of stars fill the night sky. Some stars stand out because they are very bright. Other stars appear to be grouped together. To people of long ago, these star groups seemed to form figures. We call these groups of stars *constellations*. Different people saw different things in the stars, based on how they lived and what they believed. Some people saw a dog, a lion, and a hunter with a bow and arrow. Others saw a ship, a princess, and a crab.

2   In the past, people told stories about the figures in the stars. Many of those stories explained how the constellations came to be. People found ways to use the stars, too. They knew that certain constellations appeared in specific places at certain times of the year. So farmers used the stars as a calendar to keep track of the months and seasons. Travelers used the stars as a map to find their way.

3   One of the best-known star groups is the Big Dipper. It is actually part of a constellation called Ursa Major, or the Big Bear. It has played an important role in American history, partly because it points to the North Star. If you could find the Big Dipper, you could tell which direction was north. Hundreds of years ago, explorers looking for America used it to set their course. In the 1800s, enslaved people in the South used it to find their way to the North.

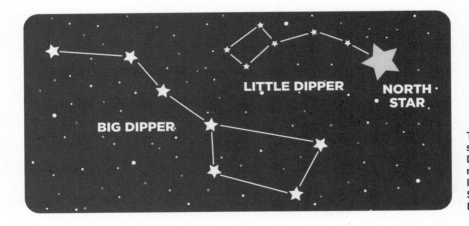

The two outer stars in the Big Dipper's bowl make a straight line with the North Star in the Little Dipper.

4   Many enslaved people could not read or write, but they could find the Big Dipper in the night sky. And from that they could locate the North Star. As the name implies, the constellation looks like a dipping ladle, or a drinking gourd. "Follow the Drinking Gourd" was the title of a folk song written in the 1900s. It told the story of people using a constellation to find their way.

(continued)

5   The National Park Service has two parks that honor the people who followed the Drinking Gourd. Both are named for Harriet Tubman, a woman who helped lead many people to freedom.

20. Which detail best shows the text structure used to organize this passage?

(A) "Some stars stand out because they are very bright. Other stars appear to be grouped together."

(B) "In the past, people told stories about the figures in the stars."

(C) "People found ways to use the stars, too."

(D) "One of the best-known star groups is the Big Dipper."

21. The North Star is part of what constellation?

(A) Leo, the Lion

(B) The Big Dipper

(C) Orion, the Hunter

(D) The Little Dipper

22. How were the constellations useful to people long ago? Choose <u>two</u> answers.

(A) as a map

(B) as a calendar

(C) as a night light

(D) as a fortune teller

(E) as a weather predictor

23. Which <u>two</u> sentences in paragraph 3 support the idea that the Big Dipper was important to American history? Underline the sentences.

One of the best-known star groups is the Big Dipper. It is actually part of a constellation called Ursa Major, or the Big Bear. It has played an important role in American history, partly because it points to the North Star. If you could find the Big Dipper, you could tell which direction was north. Hundreds of years ago, explorers looking for America used it to set their course. In the 1800s, enslaved people in the South used it to find their way to the North.

ANSWER KEY

ICE CREAM IN A BAG (page 6)

1. Salt and ice (Step 2 in the directions says, "Fill the larger gallon-size bag halfway with ice. Add the salt.")

2. D

A: Incorrect. This answer might seem reasonable, but the directions do not mention any possible harm from touching the salt.

B: Incorrect. The directions suggest wearing gloves while shaking the bag, but gloves would not keep the bag from breaking.

C: Incorrect. The berries are mixed with other ingredients in the bag, so wearing gloves will not prevent crushing them.

D: Correct. Step 4 says, "Wear gloves so your hands don't freeze."

3. B

A: Incorrect. This recipe calls for "½ cup fresh berries"; it is not intended to be used with lemons.

B: Correct. This recipe calls for "½ cup fresh berries," so it can be used to make strawberry ice cream.

C: Incorrect. This recipe calls for "½ cup fresh berries"; it cannot be used to make chocolate ice cream.

D: Incorrect. This recipe calls for "½ cup fresh berries"; it is not intended to be used with peanut butter.

CLIMBING EL CAPITAN (page 7)

1. B, D

A: Incorrect. Although this sentence suggests that El Capitan is an impressive sight, it does not explain why climbers would be drawn to it.

B: Correct. This sentence helps explain why climbers would be attracted to El Capitan: It is a challenge to climb one of the world's tallest rock walls.

C: Incorrect. This sentence suggests a reason *not* to climb El Capitan—because it is impossible—rather than a reason to climb it.

D: Correct. This sentence helps explain why climbers would be attracted to El Capitan: To prove that they can accomplish something that is not easy.

E: Incorrect. Although this sentence tells how long the climb takes, it does not explain why climbers would be drawn to El Capitan.

2. C

A: Incorrect. Although climbers may miss their family and friends while climbing, this is not the reason given in the passage.

B: Incorrect. Although climbers certainly could lose their concentration during a climb, this is not the reason given in the passage.

C: Correct. Paragraph 3 explains that a multi-day climb requires a lot of food, water, and gear, which add extra weight.

D: Incorrect. Paragraph 3 explains that climbers carry a "portaledge" for sleeping each night during the climb.

3. Sample answer: Hannold climbed El Capitan without ropes or protective gear. (Paragraph 5 states this.)

THE LITTLE MONKEY OF THE MOUNTAIN (page 9)

1. B, C

A: Incorrect. The passage mentions the continents where marsupials live but does not say anything about living near an ocean.

B: Correct. Paragraph 2 says that kangaroos and koalas are marsupials.

C: Correct. Paragraph 2 says that a marsupial mother carries her baby in a pouch.

D: Incorrect. Paragraph 4 says that the *monito del monte* eats insects, so this answer cannot be true.

E: Incorrect. Paragraph 1 explains that the *monito del monte* may be called a little monkey, but it is a marsupial; they are not the same.

2. South America (Paragraph 1 states this fact.)

3. B

A: Incorrect. Although this sentence tells what the animal's name means in English, it does not tell why the animal is special.

B: Correct. The fact that this animal is the smallest marsupial in the world makes it special.

C: Incorrect. Although this sentence tells what the animal looks like, it does not tell why the animal is special.

D: Incorrect. This sentence describes one of the animal's habits but does not tell why the animal is special.

4. A, E

A: Correct. Paragraph 4 says that the *monito del monte* eats insects.

B: Incorrect. Paragraph 4 says that the *monito del monte* can climb trees, but the passage does not say it can fly.

C: Incorrect. Paragraph 4 says that the *monito del monte* is active at night, but the passage does not say it is blind.

D: Incorrect. Paragraph 3 describes the animal's body and tail, but the passage does not mention horns.

E: Correct. Paragraph 4 says that the *monito del monte* is nocturnal.

SAILING FOR CHANGE (page 11)

1. B

A: Incorrect. Although the passage describes how Greta Thunberg approaches traveling, this is not her main concern.

B: Correct. Greta Thunberg is most worried about climate change and wants to do something about it.

C: Incorrect. Although Greta Thunberg organized school strikes when she was 15, she did so to call attention to climate change.

D: Incorrect. Although Greta Thunberg spoke to the UN, her main concern was to call attention to climate change.

2. Sample answers (pick any two): Greta Thunberg started a school strike, appeared on TV, and made speeches. (Paragraph 3 says how Greta called attention to climate change.)

3. C

A: Incorrect. Although this sentence describes an effect of Greta's speaking out, it does not explain why she went to New York.

B: Incorrect. This sentence suggests that Greta was going somewhere, but it does not explain why she went to New York.

C: Correct. This sentence explains that Greta went to New York to speak at the UN.

D: Incorrect. Although this sentence indicates that the UN is in New York, it does not explain why Greta went there.

4. D

A: Incorrect. Paragraph 2 gives this information, but this is a detail and not the central idea.

B: Incorrect. Paragraph 6 implies that Greta knows this fact, but this is a detail and not the central idea.

C: Incorrect. Paragraph 6 gives this information, but this is a detail and not the central idea.

D: Correct. This is the central idea of the passage.

5. "Fifteen days later, crowds met her in New York and cheered for her." (This sentence supports the idea that many people liked her ideas.)

A SUNKEN TREASURE (page 13)
1A. D

A: Incorrect. Although paragraph 5 gives this information, it is a detail and not the central idea.

B: Incorrect. This sentence states a main idea of paragraph 2, but it is not the central idea of the passage as a whole.

C: Incorrect. Although paragraph 2 gives this information, it is a detail and not the central idea.

D: Correct. This is the central idea of the passage.

1B. B

A: Incorrect. This is the first sentence of the passage, but it does not support the idea that an important sunken treasure was found.

B: Correct. This detail sentence supports the idea that a group of explorers found sunken treasure.

C: Incorrect. This sentence describes the lost treasure in a general way, but it is not the best support for the idea that an important sunken treasure was found.

D: Incorrect. This sentence gives historical information, but it does not support the idea that an important sunken treasure was found.

2. B

A: Incorrect. The paragraph says that the *S.S. Central America* sailed between Panama and New York, but this is a detail and not the main topic.

B: Correct. The paragraph explains that people traveled from California to New York by ship via Panama.

C: Incorrect. The paragraph gives some information about the California Gold Rush, but this is a detail and not the main topic.

D: Incorrect. This detail helps explain the route of the *S.S. Central America,* but it is not the main topic.

3. C

A: Incorrect. This detail suggests that there was gold on the ship, but it does not say it was very valuable.

B: Incorrect. This sentence describes the history of the *S.S. Central America,* but it does not say it was carrying something very valuable.

C: Correct. This detail describes the ship's very valuable cargo that sank.

D: Incorrect. This sentence suggests that the sunken ship held more treasure than had already been found, but it does not say it was very valuable.

4. A, E

A: Correct. This sentence summarizes the first three paragraphs of the passage.

B: Incorrect. This is a minor detail in the passage and should not be included in a summary.

C: Incorrect. This is a detail from the last paragraph, but it is not important enough to include in a summary.

D: Incorrect. This detail can be drawn from paragraph 2, but it is not important enough to include in a summary.

E: Correct. This sentence summarizes the discovery described in the last two paragraphs of the passage.

ANCIENT CAVE ART TELLS A STORY
(page 15)
1A. D

A: Incorrect. Although paragraphs 2 and 3 provide this information, it is a detail and not the central idea.

B: Incorrect. Paragraph 6 states that the oldest cave paintings in Europe showed handprints and circles; this is not the central idea of the passage as a whole.

C: Incorrect. Although paragraph 2 gives this information, it is a detail and not the central idea.

D: Correct. This is the central idea of the passage.

1B. C

A: Incorrect. Although this sentence supports answer choice A in Part A, it does not support the central idea that cave art found in Indonesia provides new information.

B: Incorrect. This sentence supports answer choice A in Part A, but it does not support the central idea that cave art found in Indonesia provides new information.

C: Correct. This detail supports the central idea that cave art found in Indonesia provides new information.

D: Incorrect. This sentence states a conclusion about the cave painting, but it is not the best support for the idea that cave art found in Indonesia provides new information.

2. D

A: Incorrect. The paragraph says that uranium was found in the cave art, but this is a detail and not the central idea.

B: Incorrect. The paragraph explains that artists may have added to the painting at different times, but this is a detail and not the central idea.

C: Incorrect. This is a detail given in the paragraph but not the central idea.

D: Correct. This paragraph explains how scientists determined the age of the cave art.

3. B, D

A: Incorrect. This is a generalization based on the passage, but it should not be included in a summary.

B: Correct. This sentence summarizes the first half of the passage.

C: Incorrect. This is a detail from paragraph 4, but it is not important enough to include in a summary.

D: Correct. This sentence summarizes the second half of the passage.

E: Incorrect. This detail can be drawn from paragraph 2, but it is not important enough to include in a summary.

4. B

A: Incorrect. This detail describes the size of the painting but does not support the idea that people told stories through art.

B: Correct. This detail supports the idea that people told stories through art.

C: Incorrect. This detail describes some of the figures in the painting but does not show that the painting told a story.

D: Incorrect. This detail describes the color in the painting but does not support the idea that people told stories through art.

CIRQUE DU SOLEIL (page 17)

1. D

A: Incorrect. Paragraph 2 says that Cirque du Soleil "has no animal acts," so it would not present lion taming.

B: Incorrect. Paragraph 2 says that Cirque du Soleil "has no animal acts," so people would not be likely to see elephant tricks.

C: Incorrect. The passage describes many kinds of acrobatic acts but does not mention puppetry.

D: Correct. This is the kind of acrobatic act people might see in the Cirque du Soleil.

2. B, E

A: Incorrect. The passage does not imply that the costumes are safe.

B: Correct. The passage mentions "shiny red suits," so they could be described as colorful.

C: Incorrect. The passage does not imply that the costumes are simple.

D: Incorrect. Since the passage mentions "jewels and sparkles" and "shiny red suits," the costumes would not be described as plain.

E: Correct. The passage mentions "jewels and sparkles" and "shiny red suits," so they could be described as exciting.

3. 2, 3, 1, 4 (Paragraphs 2 to 5 describe the order in which Cirque de Soleil was created.)

4. D

A: Incorrect. This sentence tells how Laliberté's group began but does not show that his dream came true.

B: Incorrect. This sentence describes the early days of Laliberté's group but does not show that his dream came true.

C: Incorrect. This sentence describes how Laliberté's group worked but does not show that his dream came true.

D: Correct. This sentence shows that Laliberté's dream came true because the circus performed shows all over the world.

GOING SOLO IN INDIA (page 19)

1. C, D

A: Incorrect. Although this sentence refers to something that Newman did, it does not show that she is a very experienced kayaker.

B: Incorrect. This sentence tells how old Newman was when she did something alone, but it does not show that she is a very experienced kayaker.

C: Correct. Winning international events and awards shows that Newman is a very experienced kayaker.

D: Correct. Exploring rivers all over the world shows that Newman is a very experienced kayaker.

E: Incorrect. Although this sentence refers to something that Newman wanted to do, it does not show that she is a very experienced kayaker.

2. Sample answer: Newman had to get permission from the Indian government before she could travel to Ladakh. (Paragraph 3 states this.)

3. B

A: Incorrect. The passage does not mention bad weather, so that was not the cause of Newman's trouble.

B: Correct. Paragraph 5 implies that Newman got into trouble on the river because she made a mistake.

C: Incorrect. Paragraph 8 explains that snow melt made the river bigger and faster, but this was not the cause of Newman's trouble.

D: Incorrect. Although Newman may have lost some of her gear when she got into trouble on the river, she did not forget any gear.

4. D

A: Incorrect. This sentence describes what might have happened if Newman lost her gear, but it does not tell why she was happy to see the children.

B: Incorrect. This sentence describes how Newman felt after she capsized, but it does not tell why she was happy to see the children.

C: Incorrect. This sentence describes how the children reacted to Newman, but it does not tell why she was happy to see them.

D: Correct. This sentence tells why Newman was happy to see the children—at a time in her journey when she felt discouraged.

5. C

A: Incorrect. Newman got trapped against a rock on the second day, so this was not the reason her trip was so challenging on the fifth day.

B: Incorrect. Newman's kayak got thrown off course on the second day, so this was not the reason her trip was so challenging on the fifth day.

C: Correct. Paragraph 8 says that snow melt had made the river bigger and faster, so this made the trip challenging on the fifth day.

D: Incorrect. Newman was prepared for a challenging trip on the fifth day, and the passage does not mention waterfalls.

8,000 MILES ON A BIKE WITH ERIK DOUDS (page 22)

1. C

A: Incorrect. Disease did not make it hard for Douds to learn to ride a bike as a child; the disease was not diagnosed until he was in high school.

B: Incorrect. The passage does not suggest that Douds did not enjoy sports, so this was not the reason he did not learn to ride a bike as a child.

C: Correct. In paragraph 4, Douds explains that he did not learn to ride a bike as a child because he lived on a steep hill.

D: Incorrect. Douds does not say that he lived in a city with a lot of traffic.

2A. D

A: Incorrect. Paragraph 7 suggests that Douds felt afraid, or worried, but it does not suggest he was angry.

B: Incorrect. When Douds described the disease and how he felt about it, he clearly understood the situation, so he was not "confused."

C: Incorrect. In paragraph 5, Douds says that his life changed forever, so he was not "bored."

D: Correct. In paragraph 7, Douds admits that he feared the disease might keep him from doing what he wanted to do.

2B. C

A: Incorrect. This sentence describes an effect of having diabetes, but it does not support the idea that he was worried when he found out he had it.

B: Incorrect. Although this sentence describes an effect of having diabetes, it does not show that Douds was worried when he found out he had it.

C: Correct. This sentence supports the idea that Douds was worried when he found out he had diabetes.

D: Incorrect. This sentence describes where Douds was during the interview, but it does not support the idea that he was worried when he found out he had diabetes.

3. A

A: Correct. In paragraph 6, Douds explains that a special device monitors his blood sugar and sends data to a phone every five minutes.

B: Incorrect. In paragraph 6, Douds mentions hiding food from bears, but technology does not help him do that.

C: Incorrect. Although technology might help Douds keep in touch with friends, he does not mention this idea in the interview.

D: Incorrect. Although technology might help Douds track his miles, he does not mention this idea in the interview.

4. Sample answer: "Start pedaling" (Based on what Douds says in paragraph 8, he would probably advise that person to just start pedaling.)

MAKE WAY FOR FUN GUY! (page 25)

1. D

A: Incorrect. The role of fungi is important to our environment, but it is not hard to understand.

B: Incorrect. Although fungi may be interesting or amusing to some people, that is not the meaning of *essential*.

C: Incorrect. Although some fungi are used to make medicines, the word *essential* does not refer to an ability to fight disease.

D: Correct. The word *essential* means "important or necessary."

2. Sample answer: "rots" or "turns rotten"

3. C

A: Incorrect. The phrase "so large" describes some kinds of mushrooms but does not give a clue to the meaning of *diet*.

B: Incorrect. The phrase "more mushrooms" refers to the American diet but does not help explain what the word means.

C: Correct. The phrase "each American eats" gives a clue to the meaning of *diet,* which refers to the foods and drinks a person regularly consumes.

D: Incorrect. The phrase "four pounds" describes an amount of mushrooms but does not give a clue to the meaning of *diet*.

4. A

A: Correct. The word *annual* means "per year" or "every year."

B: Incorrect. The passage might imply that people eat a large amount of mushrooms, but this is not the meaning of *annual*.

C: Incorrect. The phrase "all at once" could fit in the sentence, but this is not the meaning of *annual*.

D: Incorrect. The passage might imply that eating four pounds of mushrooms is hard to believe, but this is not the meaning of *annual*.

5. Sample answer: "like" or "alike"

CROSSING THE ATLANTIC (page 27)

1. Sample answer: "traded" or "sent back and forth"

2. C

A: Incorrect. Although the passage says that Cyrus Field became a rich man, this is not the meaning of *prominent*.

B: Incorrect. Although Cyrus Field may have been clever or skilled, this is not the meaning of *prominent*.

C: Correct. The word *prominent* means "well-known or important."

D: Incorrect. Cyrus Field may have been honest and hard-working, but this is not the meaning of *prominent*.

3. D

A: Incorrect. The phrase "knew nothing" refers to Field's knowledge of the telegraph, but it does not give a clue to the meaning of *invest*.

B: Incorrect. The phrase "a chance" refers to the cable project, but it does not give a clue to the meaning of *invest*.

C: Incorrect. The phrase "make money" refers to Field's goal, but it does not give a clue to the meaning of *invest*.

D: Correct. People put in money to pay for the project in hopes of getting more money back; this is the meaning of *invest*.

4. Sample answer: "become weaker," "weaken," or "change"

5. D

A: Incorrect. The phrase "caused a delay" refers to the effect of a war on the cable project, but it does not give a clue to the meaning of *jubilant*.

B: Incorrect. The phrase "succeeded in the end" describes the result of Field's efforts, but it does not give a clue to the meaning of *jubilant*.

C: Incorrect. The phrase "both sides of the ocean" describes where the people were but does not give a clue to the meaning of *jubilant*.

D: Correct. The people celebrated for days when the cable was completed because they were very happy or thrilled; that is what *jubilant* means.

AUGUSTA SAVAGE, ARTIST EXTRAORDINAIRE (page 29)

1. B

A: Incorrect. The word *persisted* means that Savage did not give up; it is almost the opposite of "ran away."

B: Correct. The word *persisted* means that Savage did not give up; she kept trying.

C: Incorrect. Although Savage may have grown quickly by working hard, that is not the meaning of *persisted*.

D: Incorrect. Savage probably did not agree with her father about being an artist, but that is not the meaning of *persisted*.

2. C

A: Incorrect. Although "completed" would fit into the sentence, that is not the meaning of *pursued*.

B: Incorrect. Although Savage earned money from her career, that is not the meaning of *pursued*.

C: Correct. The word *pursued* means "went after," or in this case, "worked toward."

D: Incorrect. Although "took a break from" would fit into the sentence, that is not the meaning of *pursued*.

3. A

A: Correct. Savage *enrolled* in an art course, meaning that she signed up for it.

B: Incorrect. Although "created art" would fit into the sentence, that is not the meaning of *enrolled*.

C: Incorrect. The phrase "studied hard" would fit into the sentence, but that is not the meaning of *enrolled*.

D: Incorrect. Although Savage probably had to pay the cost for the art course, that is not the meaning of *enrolled*.

4. C

A: Incorrect. Savage was unable to "sell her artwork" in Florida, but that phrase does not give a clue to the meaning of *influential*.

B: Incorrect. The phrase "over the next few years" describes when Savage became influential but does not give a clue to its meaning.

C: Correct. Savage was influential on other artists because she had an effect on them; she influenced them.

D: Incorrect. The Harlem Renaissance was "a movement," but that phrase does not give a clue to the meaning of *influential*.

5. Sample answer: "overseas" or "in another country"

THE FIRST DIVING MACHINE (page 31)

1. D

A: Incorrect. Although some sentences in the passage explain causes and effects, that is not the text structure used in the first paragraph.

B: Incorrect. Although the first sentence refers to "many years," the first paragraph does not present events in time order.

C: Incorrect. The author presents a problem in the first paragraph but does not compare or contrast it with anything else.

D: Correct. The problem was that Lethbridge had no way to explore underwater; his solution was to build a diving machine.

2A. A

A: Correct. After presenting a problem and solution in the first paragraph, the rest of the passage describes major events in Lethbridge's life in time order.

B: Incorrect. Although some sentences in the passage explain causes and effects, that is not the main text structure of the passage as a whole.

C: Incorrect. The first paragraph presents a problem and solution, but the passage as a whole describes events in time order.

D: Incorrect. Although Lethbridge's diving adventures were quite different from his job as a wool merchant, the author does not use comparison-contrast as a text structure.

2B. B, E

A: Incorrect. This sentence describes Lethbridge's regular job, but it does not present information in time order.

B: Correct. By referring to the year 1715, this sentence supports the text structure of describing events in time order.

C: Incorrect. This sentence describes what Lethbridge could do with his diving suit, but it does not present information in time order.

D: Incorrect. This sentence describes a drawback of Lethbridge's diving suit, but it does not present information in time order.

E: Correct. By referring to the year 1724, this sentence supports the text structure of describing events in time order.

FIGHTING WITH RESPECT (page 33)

1A. D

A: Incorrect. Although some sentences refer to events or traditions from long ago, the passage does not present information in time order.

B: Incorrect. Although some sentences explain causes and effects, this is not the text structure of the passage as a whole.

C: Incorrect. Although learning a martial art could be considered a "solution" of sorts, this is not the text structure of the passage as a whole.

D: Correct. The author compares and contrasts three forms of martial arts.

1B. D

A: Incorrect. This sentence defines the word *martial* but does not present a comparison or contrast.

B: Incorrect. This sentence explains that there are many forms of martial arts but does not present a comparison or contrast.

C: Incorrect. This sentence describes a feature of karate but does not present a comparison or contrast.

D: Correct. This sentence supports the text structure by comparing muay thai with karate.

2. C

A: Incorrect. Both muay thai and karate allow kicks.

B: Incorrect. Paragraph 8 states that both muay thai and karate are Olympic sports.

C: Correct. Karate has a traditional white uniform called a *gi,* while muay thai does not.

D: Incorrect. Neither muay thai nor karate uses weapons other than parts of the body.

3. A

A: Correct. Both muay thai and karate come from Asia, but capoeira developed in Brazil.

B: Incorrect. All three forms of martial arts have a long history, so this is not a difference.

C: Incorrect. Both muay thai and karate are Olympic sports, but capoeira is not.

D: Incorrect. All three forms of martial arts include competition, so this is not a difference.

4.

Descriptions	Karate	Muay Thai	Capoeira
Students usually wear white clothing.	X		X
It uses protective gear in the Olympics.		X	
Respect is very important.	X	X	X
Colored belts show skill levels.	X		X

THE TOUGHEST HORSE RACE IN THE WORLD (page 36)

1A. D

A: Incorrect. Although the Mongol Derby is described as being tougher than all other horse races, the author does not use comparison-contrast as a text structure.

B: Incorrect. Although some sentences explain causes and effects, this is not the main text structure of the passage as a whole.

C: Incorrect. Although the passage describes some of the problems that riders face in the Derby, this is not the main text structure of the passage as a whole.

D: Correct. From 800 years ago to today, the passage describes events in chronological order.

1B. B, E

A: Incorrect. This sentence tells about Genghis Khan's mail system, but it does not present information in time order.

B: Correct. By referring to the year the Derby began, this sentence supports the chronological text structure.

C: Incorrect. This sentence describes a requirement of the Derby, but it does not present information in time order.

D: Incorrect. This sentence compares the horses used in the Derby with those used long ago, but it does not present information in time order.

E: Correct. By referring to the year when Prior-Palmer won the Derby, this sentence supports the chronological text structure.

2. A

A: Correct. In both the Derby and the mail system, riders stopped at stations along the way to change horses.

B: Incorrect. Riders pay a fee to enter the Derby, but the description of Khan's mail system does not mention cost.

C: Incorrect. Riders in Khan's mail system were men, but the Derby allows both men and women.

D: Incorrect. Taking mail across Mongolia took a few weeks, but the Derby must be completed in 10 days.

3. C

A: Incorrect. Although this sentence says how many racers enter each year, it does not explain why riding across it is so challenging.

B: Incorrect. Although this sentence describes where Mongolia is, it does not explain why riding across it is so challenging.

C: Correct. Mongolia's "wild landscapes" make the Derby challenging because riders have to handle many kinds of terrain.

D: Incorrect. Although this sentence explains when racers can ride, it does not explain why riding across Mongolia is so challenging.

4. "The course itself is not marked, so riders have to find their own way." (The conjunction *so* indicates that this sentence has a cause and an effect.)

GRANDMA MOSES (page 39)

1. B

A: Incorrect. Although the author gives some information about what Grandma Moses did on her farm, this is not the author's main purpose.

B: Correct. The author's main purpose is to tell about Grandma Moses's life and work.

C: Incorrect. Although the author notes that Grandma Moses lived on a farm and later started to paint, the passage does not explain how she learned.

D: Incorrect. Although the author describes Grandma Moses as "one of the best-loved people in America," the passage does not compare her work to that of other artists.

2. "She was a remarkable artist and one of the best-loved people in America." (The other sentences in the paragraph give facts about Grandma Moses, but the last sentence expresses the author's view of her as "remarkable.")

3. C, D

A: Incorrect. These sentences describe how an art dealer discovered Grandma Moses but do not tell what he thought of her work.

B: Incorrect. This sentence gives the author's description of Grandma Moses's work but does not tell what people thought of it.

C: Correct. These sentences state that many people "loved" Grandma Moses's work.

D: Correct. This sentence notes that other people thought of Grandma Moses's work as too simple and child-like.

E: Incorrect. This sentence describes how many people felt about Grandma Moses's death but not what they thought of her work.

CALBUCO VOLCANO ERUPTS / A VIEW OF CALBUCO (page 41)

1. C

A: Incorrect. Although Text A tells what happened, it does not explain why the volcano erupted.

B: Incorrect. Although Text A mentions that people had to evacuate the area, it does not try to convince people to move away.

C: Correct. Text A presents the facts about the eruption, as a news article would.

D: Incorrect. Although Text A describes what happened, it does not describe the people in the area.

2. A

A: Correct. Both texts mention that people had to leave the area when the volcano erupted.

B: Incorrect. Text B notes that the roads were buried in ash, but Text A does not mention the roads.

C: Incorrect. The writer of Text B notes that one corner of his roof fell in, but Text A does not mention this.

D: Incorrect. The writer of Text B mentions his dogs, but Text A does not say anything about dogs barking.

3. B, E

A: Incorrect. Both texts describe the town of Ensenada, so this is not a difference.

B: Correct. Text B is a personal narrative written by Pablo Saumann; Text A is a news article written in third person.

C: Incorrect. Both texts give the date of April 22, so this is not a difference.

D: Incorrect. Both texts mention that no one was hurt, so this is not a difference.

E: Correct. The writer of Text B expresses his feelings about what happened, but Text A reports only the facts.

4. C

A: Incorrect. This sentence describes the moment when Saumann could return home but does not tell how he felt.

B: Incorrect. This sentence describes how Saumann returned home but does not tell how he felt.

C: Correct. This sentence tells how Saumann felt ("amazed") when he got home.

D: Incorrect. This sentence describes what Saumann saw when he returned home but does not tell how he felt.

5. A

A: Correct. The last paragraph says, "I still love my backyard paradise."

B: Incorrect. Saumann does not know if the volcano will erupt again; he says it is "quiet—for now."

C: Incorrect. Saumann refers to the townspeople as "us," but he does not mention friends or family as a reason to stay in Ensenada.

D: Incorrect. Saumann may have experienced some excitement during the event, but he does not mention excitement or danger as a reason to stay in Ensenada.

RAPA NUI / A MYSTERY SOLVED (page 44)

1. D

A: Incorrect. Although the author describes how people got to Rapa Nui, his purpose is not to tell how the island was formed.

B: Incorrect. Although the author makes the island sound interesting and worthy of a visit, he does not try to convince people to go there.

C: Incorrect. The author notes that the moai were all carved in one quarry, but his purpose is not to explain how they were carved.

D: Correct. The author's main purpose is to describe the moai on the island.

2. "To see them gives one a sense of awe." (The other sentences in the first paragraph give factual information, but this sentence reveals the author's view that the moai give a person a "sense of awe.")

3. A

A: Correct. Text A describes the moai, but Text B explains why they were carved and what they mean.

B: Incorrect. Although Text B describes work done in the past few years, its purpose is not to compare the past and present.

C: Incorrect. Although Text B describes some aspects of growing crops on the island, its purpose is to explain why the moai were created.

D: Incorrect. Although Text B mentions "the scientists" who studied the moai, it does not give any description of them.

4. "But over many decades, the people foolishly cut down all of the trees on the island." (The word *foolishly* suggests the author's critical view of what the people did.)

5. C

A: Incorrect. Although the statues are large and imposing, they were not carved to scare people away.

B: Incorrect. The statues were placed on certain spots of soil, but they were not intended to keep the soil from washing away.

C: Correct. Paragraph 6 explains that the moai "honored the soil and helped it produce food."

D: Incorrect. Text A suggests that the statues may have represented important people who died, but Text B gives a different explanation.

REMEMBERING THE *HINDENBURG* (page 47)

1. 3 days (The timeline shows that the *Hindenburg* left Germany on May 3 and arrived in the U.S. on May 6.)

2. Greenland (The map shows that the *Hindenburg* passed over Greenland.)

3. D

A: Incorrect. According to the timeline, the *Hindenburg* left from Frankfurt but landed in Lakehurst.

B: Incorrect. The timeline and the map show that the *Hindenburg* flew over Boston, but it did not land there.

C: Incorrect. The passage, the map, and the timeline all indicate that the *Hindenburg* flew over New York City, but it did not land there.

D: Correct. According to the timeline, the *Hindenburg* landed in Lakehurst, New Jersey.

4A. B

A: Incorrect. Although the *Hindenburg* had reached its destination, the passage does not suggest that it was low on fuel.

B: Correct. Paragraph 3 says that the pilot had to delay the landing, so he circled over New York City.

C: Incorrect. Although the weather was not very good, the passage does not say that the pilot could not see the airport.

D: Incorrect. Some passengers may have wanted to see New York City, but that is not the reason the *Hindenburg* circled over it.

4B. C

A: Incorrect. This sentence tells when the *Hindenburg* left Germany but does not tell why it had to circle over New York City on May 6.

B: Incorrect. This sentence tells how many people were on the *Hindenburg*, but it does not tell why it had to circle over New York City on May 6.

C: Correct. This sentence implies that the *Hindenburg* had to delay its landing and circle over New York City due to bad weather.

D: Incorrect. This sentence describes what the pilot did during the landing, but it does not tell why the *Hindenburg* had to circle over New York City on May 6.

5. "The age of airships came to an end." (Because of the disaster, the *Hindenburg* was the last airship to fly to the United States, and the age of airships came to an end.)

THE BEES OF NOTRE-DAME (page 50)

1. D

A: Incorrect. Many buildings were made of stone, so this is not something special about Notre-Dame.

B: Incorrect. This feature may be considered "special" today, but there were no beehives on the roof when Notre-Dame was built.

C: Incorrect. Although Notre-Dame had stained-glass windows, these are not mentioned in the passage; and many other churches had stained-glass windows, so this is not something special about Notre-Dame.

D: Correct. The sidebar, "Notre-Dame Facts," notes that it was the tallest building in Europe when it was built.

2. 12 million people (The sidebar, "Notre-Dame Facts," states this fact.)

3. "Smoke from the fire must have put the bees to sleep. They stayed in their hives until the fire went out." (These two sentences explain that smoke put the bees to sleep so they stayed in their beehives and were not harmed.)

4. Sample answers: more than 100 years, or 107 years (The sidebar, "Notre-Dame Facts," notes that construction began in 1163 and ended about 1270.)

5. B

A: Incorrect. This sentence says that bees were living at Notre-Dame but does not explain why they were there.

B: Correct. This sentence explains that bees were living at Notre-Dame because the city government placed hives there.

C: Incorrect. This sentence describes a result of the bees living at Notre-Dame but does not explain why they were there.

D: Incorrect. This sentence explains that Geant takes care of the bees living at Notre-Dame but does not explain why they were there.

A LANGUAGE OF HOPE (page 52)

1. C

A: Incorrect. Paragraph 2 says that Zamenhof was an eye doctor, but that was not the reason he wanted to invent a new language.

B: Incorrect. Although paragraph 2 says that Zamenhof grew up in Poland, that was not the reason he wanted to invent a new language.

C: Correct. Paragraph 2 says that people in Bialystok came from different backgrounds, spoke different languages, and did not understand one another.

D: Incorrect. Although paragraph 2 mentions language and learning, it does not describe the schools in Bialystok.

2. B, D

A: Incorrect. Paragraph 3 notes that Esperanto had 920 word roots, but that was not a feature that made it easy to learn.

B: Correct. Paragraph 4 explains that Esperanto had all regular verbs, which made the language easier to learn than most other languages.

C: Incorrect. Although people in different places who learned the language could understand it, this was not a feature that made it easy to learn.

D: Correct. Paragraph 4 explains that every word in Esperanto was spelled as it was pronounced, which made the language easier to learn than most other languages.

E: Incorrect. Paragraph 4 notes that Esperanto had 34 sounds, but that was not a feature that made it easier to learn than other languages.

3. "The language itself was based mainly on European languages." (People in China or Egypt would not speak European languages, so a language "based mainly on European languages" might be difficult to learn.)

4. Sample answers: 100,000 or 2 million (The last paragraph in the passage says that some sources estimate the number of Esperanto speakers at 2 million; others estimate 100,000. The actual number is probably somewhere in between.)

5. Spanish (The chart in the sidebar shows it is the second-most widely spoken language.)

6. B

A: Incorrect. The chart in the sidebar shows that 119 million people speak Lahnda.

B: Correct. The chart in the sidebar shows that 379 million people speak English.

C: Incorrect. The chart in the sidebar shows that 460 million people speak Spanish.

D: Incorrect. The text in the sidebar says that 3.6 billion people speak one of the top ten languages.

GOT BUGS? (page 55)

1. B

A: Incorrect. Although paragraph 2 says that the world's population keeps growing, this is not the author's main argument.

B: Correct. This is the author's main point in the passage, and she provides reasons to support her argument.

C: Incorrect. Although paragraph 5 mentions climate change as a supporting detail, this is not the author's main argument.

D: Incorrect. Paragraph 5 makes this point, but it is not the author's main argument.

2. Sample answers (pick any two): beetles, moths, bees, ants, grasshoppers, termites, and grubs (Paragraph 3 states these facts.)

3. "More than 2 billion people in more than 100 countries already eat bugs." (This sentence in paragraph 3 gives evidence to support the idea that many people eat bugs.)

4. C, D, F

A: Incorrect. Although this sentence suggests that grasshoppers taste good, it does not support the main argument that we should eat more insects.

B: Incorrect. Although the UN report supports the author's main argument, this sentence does not give a reason to eat more insects.

C: Correct. This sentence supports the main argument by stating that insects are good for your health.

D: Correct. This sentence supports the main argument by showing that raising insects for food is easy and inexpensive.

E: Incorrect. Although this sentence suggests that insects don't have to be raised on a farm, it does not support the main argument that we should eat more insects.

F: Correct. This sentence supports the main argument by pointing out that eating more insects can slow or prevent climate change.

WHAT TIME IS NOON? (page 57)

1. C

A: Incorrect. This sentence gives an example of the world's time differences, but it does not support the claim that these differences did not matter for centuries.

B: Incorrect. Although this sentence notes that the world has time differences, it does not support the claim that these differences did not matter for centuries.

C: Correct. This sentence supports the claim that time differences did not matter for centuries.

D: Incorrect. Although this sentence describes how people felt about time in a general way, it is not the best explanation of why time differences did not matter for centuries.

2. "The railroads needed a way to coordinate times in different places." (This sentence explains that time zones were created because railroads crossed the country, through places where times varied, and needed to coordinate their schedules.)

3. 3:00 P.M. (The map shows that Phoenix is two hours behind Atlanta.)

4. "The Chinese decided that having one time zone would make everyone in the country feel connected." (Even though China is large enough to have several time zones, it decided to unify the country by having only one.)

ADAPTED FROM "THE MOON SPEECH," BY PRESIDENT JOHN F. KENNEDY (page 59)

1. B

A: Incorrect. Although Kennedy praises American satellites in paragraph 6, this is not his main argument.

B: Correct. This is Kennedy's main argument.

C: Incorrect. Kennedy mentions the high cost of space travel in paragraph 9, but this is not his main argument.

D: Incorrect. Although Kennedy makes this promise in paragraph 1, this is not his main argument.

2. "And we have vowed that we shall see it governed by a banner of freedom and peace." (Kennedy speaks of going to the moon first, but his goal for the moon itself is that it shall be free and peaceful, i.e., not controlled by some other government.)

3. A, D

A: Correct. Paragraph 6 states that Transit satellites helped U.S. ships navigate.

B: Incorrect. Although Kennedy implies that other countries are competing with the U.S., he does not mention the use of satellites as weapons.

C: Incorrect. Kennedy predicts that satellites will someday give warnings about forest fires and icebergs, but these benefits had not yet occurred.

D: Correct. Paragraph 6 states that *Tiros* satellites provided warnings of hurricanes and storms.

E: Incorrect. Although some satellites helped ships navigate, Kennedy does not mention using them to measure distances.

4A. D

A: Incorrect. Kennedy actually says the opposite, in paragraph 9—that the space program will cost "a good deal of money."

B: Incorrect. Although Kennedy says in paragraph 8 that the space program has created many new jobs, he does not claim that it will make the country rich.

C: Incorrect. Kennedy says near the end of the speech that getting to the moon will happen "before the end of this decade," but that would be more than two or three years.

D: Correct. Kennedy supports his main argument about going to the moon by describing the many benefits it will bring to the country and to all people.

4B. C, D

A: Incorrect. Although this sentence gives a reason to go to the moon, it does not support the idea that the space program will benefit the country in many ways.

B: Incorrect. Although this sentence promises that great progress will be made, it does not support the idea that the space program will benefit the country in many ways.

C: Correct. This sentence supports the idea that the space program will benefit the country by pointing out that it will improve our science and education.

D: Correct. **This sentence supports the idea that the space program will benefit the country by pointing out that it has already created new companies and new jobs.**

E: Incorrect. Although this sentence describes the cost of the space program, it does not show that the space program will benefit the country in many ways.

HOT! HOT! HOT! (page 62)

1. B

A: Incorrect. Paragraph 1 says that some chili peppers can make you cry, but the sidebar focuses on a pepper that can burn your skin.

B: Correct. The sidebar focuses on the Carolina Reaper, a pepper that can burn your skin.

C: Incorrect. Paragraph 1 says that some chili peppers can make you sweat, but the sidebar focuses on a pepper that can burn your skin.

D: Incorrect. Paragraph 4 says that some chili peppers can clear a stuffy nose, but the sidebar focuses on a pepper that can burn your skin.

2. "And new types are being developed all the time." (This sentence claims that new types of peppers are being developed all the time, and the sidebar describes a new kind of pepper developed in 2013.)

3. Sample answer: The Carolina Reaper is much hotter than any other pepper and has topped the list since 2013. (The second sentence in the sidebar gives this information.)

4. A

A: Correct. The sidebar provides this information, but the main passage does not mention capsaicin.

B: Incorrect. Paragraph 4 presents this information, but the sidebar does not mention it.

C: Incorrect. Paragraph 2 states this fact, but the sidebar does not mention it.

D: Incorrect. This information is implied in the sidebar, but it is also presented in paragraph 2.

SLOVENIA: A LAND OF FAIRY TALES (page 64)

1. "Even the cities seem to dwell in magical forests." ("Magical forests" are often associated with fairy tales.)

2. A, D

A: Correct. The Soca River flows through a valley in Slovenia.

B: Incorrect. Although Slovenia has a border on the Adriatic Sea, it is not the only country that does.

C: Incorrect. Part of Slovenia borders the Alps, but the Alps can be found in other countries, too.

D: Correct. The Postojna Cave is unique to Slovenia.

E: Incorrect. Although the passage says that Slovenia has underground lakes, there is no reason to think it is the only country that has them.

3. C

A: Incorrect. The Krizna Jama cave system is described in paragraph 5, but it is not mentioned in the sidebar.

B: Incorrect. The Reka River is described in paragraph 5, but it is not mentioned in the sidebar.

C: Correct. The Postojna Cave is described in the sidebar, but it is not mentioned in the main passage.

D: Incorrect. Ljubljana's castle is mentioned in paragraph 6, but it is not mentioned in the sidebar.

4. B

A: Incorrect. This fact is mentioned in paragraph 5, so it is not something the sidebar adds.

B: Correct. The sidebar describes the olm, a unique animal that is not mentioned in the passage.

C: Incorrect. This fact is mentioned in the main passage, so it is not something the sidebar adds.

D: Incorrect. Paragraph 6 mentions this fact, so it is not something the sidebar adds.

5. Sample answers (pick any two): The baby dragons are blind, their skin glows, they can survive up to 10 years without food, and they can live up to 100 years. (The sidebar describes these features that make olms unusual.)

VERY STRANGE MARATHONS (page 66)

1. B, C

A: Incorrect. Paragraph 3 mentions heat and dust as factors in 1904, but these factors are not mentioned in the description of the 1896 marathon.

B: Correct. The third-place finisher (1896) and first-place finisher (1904) were disqualified for riding in a vehicle for part of the race.

C: Correct. In both marathons, about half of the runners quit before finishing the race.

D: Incorrect. Only 17 runners entered the 1896 marathon, but 32 runners entered in 1904.

E: Incorrect. Paragraph 4 mentions a danger from wild dogs in St. Louis in 1904, but dangerous areas are not mentioned in the description of the 1896 marathon.

2. D

A: Incorrect. Although the sidebar mentions that sleep is important, the passage does not suggest that the runners lacked sleep or rest.

B: Incorrect. Neither the passage nor the sidebar mentions running shoes or clothing as a reason the runners did not finish.

C: Incorrect. The passage mentions dust as a factor in 1904, but it is not mentioned as a factor in 1896 and is not discussed in the sidebar.

D: Correct. Paragraph 2 says that most of the runners had not run long distances before, and the sidebar says that at least a year of training is recommended.

3. A

A: Correct. The sidebar stresses the importance of hydration, and the passage says the runners in St. Louis had difficulties because of the heat, the dust, and the lack of water.

B: Incorrect. The sidebar does not mention foot problems, and there is no evidence to suggest that the runners got blisters in the 1904 marathon.

C: Incorrect. The sidebar says that mental training can help runners endure pain, but there is no evidence to suggest that the runners got sore knees in the 1904 marathon.

D: Incorrect. Neither the passage nor the sidebar mentions dealing with cold weather.

4. Sample answer: Eat snacks that are easy to digest. (Paragraph 4 says that Carbajal got cramps from eating green apples, so he could have benefited from the tip about eating foods that are easy to digest.)

2,000 YEARS OF FIREWORKS (page 68)

1. China (Paragraph 2 says that fireworks were most likely invented in China 2,000 years ago, so that is where the first fireworks were set off.)

2. "When heated, air pockets in the bamboo make loud popping noises." (This sentence explains that bamboo was used to make fireworks because it made a loud popping noise when heated.)

3. C

A: Incorrect. Paragraph 4 says that the "green men" entertained the crowd by telling jokes, but that is not the reason they wore caps made from leaves.

B: Incorrect. Paragraph 4 says that Italians added salts to fireworks in the 1830s, but the salts were not in the leaves used to make caps.

C: Correct. Paragraph 4 says that the caps protected the "green men" from sparks produced by the fireworks.

D: Incorrect. Salts added to the fireworks produced color; the leaves were used to make protective hats.

A WILD WEST TOWN (page 69)

1. B

A: Incorrect. Bodey may have lived in the area for a while, but that is not the reason the town was named after him.

B: Correct. Paragraph 2 says the town was named in Bodey's honor after he found gold there.

C: Incorrect. Bodey died before the town was built, so that is not the reason the town was named after him.

D: Incorrect. Although Bodey died in a snowstorm, the town was named after him because he found gold there.

2. "Where the earth tore away, the miners found a large vein of pure gold." (This sentence explains that people hurried to Bodie because they heard that miners had found gold.)

3. D

A: Incorrect. Although Bodie had a large mining pit, that was not the reason it became known as a "wild town."

B: Incorrect. More than 8,000 people moved to Bodie for the gold, but that was not the reason it became known as a "wild town."

C: Incorrect. Paragraph 3 says that the town had a union hall for "meetings, shows, dances, and funerals," but that was not the reason it became known as a "wild town."

D: Correct. Paragraph 4 says that Bodie was a dangerous place filled with "lawbreakers," which implies that many people did not obey the laws.

4. A, B

A: Correct. This sentence from paragraph 5 gives one reason the people wanted to save Bodie.

B: Correct. This sentence from paragraph 5 explains that people wanted to save Bodie so others could see what life was like in an old mining town.

C: Incorrect. Although this sentence tells what visitors can do in Bodie, it does not tell why people wanted to save it.

D: Incorrect. Although this sentence describes what Bodie looks like today, it does not tell why people wanted to save it.

E: Incorrect. This sentence suggests that people might still want to go to Bodie to search for gold, but it does not tell why people wanted to save the town itself.

ANIMAL INVADERS (page 71)

1. B, D

A: Incorrect. The passage says that rats invaded Hawaii, but it does not mention rats in Australia.

B: Correct. Paragraph 4 says that British settlers brought camels to Australia and then later released them.

C: Incorrect. Although paragraph 1 mentions turtle eggs in Hawaii, there is no mention of turtles in Australia.

D: Correct. Paragraph 5 says that British settlers brought rabbits to Australia and the rabbit population grew rapidly.

E: Incorrect. Paragraph 3 says that Puerto Rico had a problem with cane beetles, but it does not mention cane beetles in Australia.

2. "But the farmers did not know that mongooses hunted during the day, while the rats came out only at night." (This sentence explains why bringing mongooses to Hawaii did not solve the rat problem.)

3. Carp or Asian carp (Paragraph 6 says that Asian carp are causing problems in the Mississippi River.)

4. B

A: Incorrect. Although this sentence explains why these animals are called "invasive," it does not specify why the animals cause damage to their new homes.

B: Correct. The invasive animals cause damage in their new homes because they cannot be controlled.

C: Incorrect. Although this sentence describes the scope of the problem, it does not tell why invasive animals cause so much damage.

D: Incorrect. This sentence suggests a course of action for the future, but it does not tell why invasive animals cause so much damage.

PRACTICE TEST (page 73)

The practice test has 23 questions for a total of 30 points.

1. D *[purpose and point of view]*

A: Incorrect. Although the passage describes many aspects of juggling, it does not explain how to do it.

B: Incorrect. Although paragraph 1 describes jugglers in a circus, telling a story about the circus is not the main purpose of the passage.

C: Incorrect. Even though paragraph 4 suggests giving juggling a try, this is not the main purpose of the passage.

D: Correct. The main purpose of the passage is to inform readers about juggling.

2. B *[reasons and evidence]*

A: Incorrect. This detail shows that juggling has been around for thousands of years, but it does not support the idea that it was used for war.

B: Correct. This detail describes how a Chinese warrior used juggling before a battle.

C: Incorrect. This sentence shows that ancient Romans enjoyed juggling, but it does not support the idea that it was used for war.

D: Incorrect. This sentence indicates that people in ancient Rome hired jugglers for entertainment, but it does not show that juggling was used for war.

3. C [word meaning]

A: Incorrect. Although juggling may be part of a circus, this is not the meaning of *pastime*.

B: Incorrect. This phrase could fit into the sentence, but it is not the meaning of *pastime*.

C: Correct. A *pastime* is a hobby, or "something fun to do."

D: Incorrect. Although the parts of the word may suggest honoring a "past time," this is not the meaning of *pastime*.

4. A, C [details and inferences]

A: Correct. Paragraph 3 says that juggling is a good exercise for the arms and shoulders.

B: Incorrect. Although a Chinese warrior once used juggling to intimidate the enemy, the ability to scare people is not a benefit of juggling.

C: Correct. Paragraph 3 says that juggling is a great tool for relaxation.

D: Incorrect. Although paragraph 3 says that juggling can improve eye-hand coordination, it does not claim that juggling can improve eyesight.

E: Incorrect. Although people may laugh at some juggling acts, this is not a benefit of juggling as a personal hobby.

5A. B [central ideas]

A: Incorrect. Although paragraph 2 gives this information, it is a detail and not the central idea.

B: Correct. This is the central idea of the passage.

C: Incorrect. Although paragraph 3 gives this information, it is a detail and not the central idea.

D: Incorrect. Although paragraph 4 discusses the animal's distinctive horns, this is not the central idea.

5B. C [central ideas and supporting details]

A: Incorrect. The fact that pronghorns are native to the American prairies does not support the idea that they are unique, since other animals are also native to the prairies.

B: Incorrect. The fact that pronghorns open their mouths to get more oxygen as they run does not make them unique, since other animals would do the same.

C: Correct. Being the only animal in the world with this characteristic shows that the pronghorn is unique.

D: Incorrect. A diet of grass and shrubs does not make the pronghorn unique, since other animals eat the same foods.

6. A [word meaning]

A: Correct. The pronghorn *resembles*, or "looks like," a deer.

B: Incorrect. Although the pronghorn does differ from a deer, this is not the meaning of *resembles*.

C: Incorrect. Although this phrase could fit into the sentence, it is not the meaning of *resembles*.

D: Incorrect. The pronghorn does run faster than a deer, but this is not the meaning of *resembles*.

7. C, D [analyzing events and ideas]

A: Incorrect. Although this may be true in some animals, it is not true of all horns and antlers.

B: Incorrect. The passage does not mention the color of horns or antlers, so there is no support for this as a difference.

C: Correct. Paragraph 4 describes this difference.

D: Correct. Paragraph 4 explains this difference.

E: Incorrect. Since both horns and antlers have points, they are likely sharp, so this is not an accurate difference.

8. D [purpose and point of view]

A: Incorrect. This sentence describes a characteristic of pronghorns but does not express the author's view.

B: Incorrect. Although this sentence describes a characteristic of pronghorns, it does not express the author's view.

C: Incorrect. This sentence gives factual information about pronghorns but does not express the author's view.

D: Correct. This sentence expresses the author's view of pronghorns as "awesome."

9A. B [central ideas]

A: Incorrect. Although this statement may be true, the central idea concerns the animals that *can* live in the deep ocean.

B: Correct. This is the central idea of the passage.

C: Incorrect. This statement expresses a general opinion about the deep ocean, but it is not the central idea of the passage.

D: Incorrect. Paragraph 2 gives this information, but it is a detail rather than the central idea.

9B. C [central ideas and supporting details]

A: Incorrect. This sentence expresses an opinion about ocean creatures but does not support the idea that these animals have adapted to living in the deep sea.

B: Incorrect. This sentence describes the deep sea but does not support the idea that some animals have adapted to living there.

C: Correct. This sentence gives an example of how some animals have adapted to living in the deep sea.

D: Incorrect. Although this statement is true, it does not support the idea that some animals have adapted to living in the deep sea.

10. D [reasons and evidence]

A: Incorrect. This sentence describes bioluminescence but does not show that some creatures use it to catch food.

B: Incorrect. Although this sentence explains how bioluminescence works, it does not show that some creatures use it to catch food.

C: Incorrect. This sentence gives an example of a creature that uses bioluminescence but does not show that it is used to catch food.

D: Correct. This sentence shows how bioluminescence is used to catch food.

11. "Some jellyfish can turn a bright flash on and off to confuse or scare predators." (This sentence tells how jellyfish use bioluminescence to scare predators away.) [analyzing events and ideas]

12. B [word meaning]

A: Incorrect. Although the passage says that some fish have a "large mouth" to catch prey, this phrase does not give a clue to the meaning of *sparse*.

B: Correct. The meaning of *sparse* is "scarce," so food is "hard to find."

C: Incorrect. Some fish can eat prey "in one bite," but this phrase does not give a clue to the meaning of *sparse*.

D: Incorrect. Although some fish have very long teeth, this does not give a clue to the meaning of *sparse*.

13. A *[integrating information]*

A: Correct. Both the sidebar and the passage explain that sunlight does not reach the deep ocean, so it is always dark.

B: Incorrect. The sidebar makes this statement, but the passage does not.

C: Incorrect. The passage includes this information, but the sidebar does not.

D: Incorrect. Although the passage gives this information, the sidebar does not.

14. B *[word meaning]*

A: Incorrect. New technology can help explorers dive deeper in the ocean, but it can't make them do it; this is not the meaning of *enables*.

B: Correct. New technology *enables*, or "allows," explorers to dive deeper in the ocean.

C: Incorrect. New technology can help explorers dive deeper in the ocean, but it does not teach them to do so; this is not the meaning of *enables*.

D: Incorrect. This is almost the opposite of *enables*, which means "allows" or "makes able."

15. C *[text structures]*

A: Incorrect. Although the "Other Discoveries" section describes a number of different things found in the ocean, it presents information in chronological order.

B: Incorrect. Although some things found in the deep ocean might seem like "problems," the "Other Discoveries" section presents information in chronological order.

C: Correct. By giving the dates of different discoveries, this section presents information in chronological order.

D: Incorrect. Although some sentences in this section suggest causes, it presents most of the information in chronological order.

16. C *[using sources]*

A: Incorrect. The coral garden was found near Greenland, but the train graveyard was not.

B: Incorrect. The Molloy Trench is located in the Arctic Ocean, but the train graveyard was not found there.

C: Correct. The caption says that the train graveyard was found off the coast of New Jersey.

D: Incorrect. The *Apollo 11* engines were found off the coast of Florida, but the train graveyard was not.

17. A, E *[integrating information]*

A: Correct. Both passages support this statement.

B: Incorrect. Passage D includes this idea, but Passage C does not mention Vescovo.

C: Incorrect. Passage C includes this idea, but Passage D does not mention bioluminescence.

D: Incorrect. Passage D includes this idea, but Passage C does not mention coral gardens.

E: Correct. Both passages present this information.

18. D *[integrating information]*

A: Incorrect. Both passages state that new technology will help ocean explorers, so this is not a difference.

B: Incorrect. Passage D actually describes the Five Deeps Expedition, but Passage C does not.

C: Incorrect. Both passages give information about Challenger Deep, so this is not a difference.

D: Correct. Passage C focuses on deep-sea creatures, but Passage D mainly describes objects found in the deep sea, so this is a difference.

19. D *[purpose and point of view]*

A: Incorrect. Since both authors discuss the remarkable nature and value of these expeditions, neither would be likely to agree with this point of view.

B: Incorrect. Passage D mentions trash that Vescovo found, but there is no evidence to think that both authors would agree that there is trash everywhere in the ocean.

C: Incorrect. The author of Passage D might agree with this viewpoint, but the author of Passage C focuses on the strangeness of deep-sea creatures.

D: Correct. Both passages make this statement, so the authors would likely both agree with this viewpoint.

20. B *[text structures]*

A: Incorrect. This detail presents a comparison of stars, but the overall passage is not organized by comparison-contrast.

B: Correct. This detail supports the text structure, which presents information mainly in time order, from "long ago" to "the past" to "the 1800s" to present day.

C: Incorrect. This detail suggests a problem-solution structure, but the overall passage is organized by time order.

D: Incorrect. This detail could suggest a comparison of star groups, but the overall passage is not organized by comparison-contrast.

21. D *[using sources]*

A: Incorrect. The passage says that some people saw a lion in the stars, but the North Star is not part of Leo.

B: Incorrect. Although the passage says that the Big Dipper points to the North Star, the illustration shows that the North Star is part of the Little Dipper.

C: Incorrect. Although the passage says that some people saw a hunter in the stars, the North Star is not part of Orion.

D: Correct. The illustration shows that the North Star is part of the Little Dipper.

22. A, B *[details and inferences]*

A: Correct. Paragraph 2 explains that some people "used the stars as a map to find their way."

B: Correct. Paragraph 2 explains that farmers "used the stars as a calendar to keep track of the months and seasons."

C: Incorrect. Although the stars might provide some light at night, there is no evidence in the passage to support this idea.

D: Incorrect. Some people may have tried to tell fortunes through the stars (for example, through astrology), but the passage does not mention this idea.

E: Incorrect. Although some people used the stars to mark the seasons, there is no evidence in the passage to suggest that people used them to predict the weather.

23. "Hundreds of years ago, explorers looking for America used it to set their course. In the 1800s, enslaved people in the South used it to find their way to the North." (These sentences support the idea that the Big Dipper was important to American history.) *[reasons and evidence]*